The Low-Fat Bed & Breakfast Cookbook

300 TRIED-AND-TRUE RECIPES FROM NORTH AMERICAN B&Bs

M.J. SMITH, RD

CHRONIMED PUBLISHING

The Low-Fat Bed & Breakfast Cookbook: 300
Tried and True Recipes from North American
B&Bs © 1998 by M.J. Smith, RD

Library of Congress Cataloging-in-Publication Data
Smith, M.J.
The low-fat bed & breakfast cookbook /
by M.J. Smith

      p.   cm.

Includes index.

ISBN 1-56561-149-7; $13.95

Acquiring Editor: Cheryl Kimball
Copy Editor: Jolene Steffer
Text Design & Production: David Enyeart
Illustrations: Pat Rouse
Art/Production Manager: Claire Lewis
Cover Design: Terry Dugan Design
Printed in the United States

Published by
Chronimed Publishing
P.O. Box 59032
Minneapolis, MN 55459-0032

10   9   8   7   6   5   4   3   2   1

...dedicated to innkeepers
Julie Metcalf Cull and Mary Metcalf Huser,
the dearest friends a guest could know.

To Linda B—
Happy Birthday
2002 !
love Margie

Contents

* * *

About the Author

M.J. Smith is a Registered Dietitian, cookbook author, working mother, and volunteer Stephen Minister. Her travels include favorite bed and breakfast inns in Iowa, Texas, Wisconsin, Minnesota, Mississippi, Illinois, Louisiana, Ireland, England, Germany, France, and the Czech Republic.

Ms. Smith's career as a dietitian has included teaching at the university level, self-publishing a monthly menu and recipe service, and consulting with hospitals and food businesses. She has written nine cookbooks including, *All American Low-Fat & No-Fat Meals in Minutes.* This best-selling cookbook ushered in '90s style low-fat cooking. Her subsequent titles include: *366 Low-Fat Brand-Name Recipes in Minutes, The Miracle Foods Cookbook, Year-Round Low-Fat & No-Fat Holiday Meals in Minutes,* and *Around the World Low-Fat & No-Fat Meals in Minutes.* Her 1996 hardcover book, *Diabetic Low-Fat & No-Fat Meals in Minutes* received a Bronze Medal from the National Health Information Award competition. In 1997, the Christian daybook *Daily Bread* was published to encourage readers toward a peaceful relationship with food.

M.J. Smith has been featured in *Good Housekeeping, Essence, Shape, The Lutheran, Good Taste, The Des Moines Register, The Minneapolis Star Tribune,* and *USA Today*, and has been on countless national and regional radio programs. She currently serves as the dietitian for Dick's Supermarkets, a group of fine grocery stores in Wisconsin and Illinois. Readers are encouraged to visit the author's home page at www.lowfatkitchen.com, which provides daily menus and recipes. Her e-mail address is mj@lowfatkitchen.com.

Ms. Smith is married to Dr. Andy Smith, a family physician. They have two school-aged children and live in Guttenberg, Iowa, a beautiful spot along the bluffed banks of the upper Mississippi River.

* * *

Foreword

M.J. Smith's *Low-Fat Bed and Breakfast Cookbook* provides the reader with a three dimensional dining experience to rival *The Canterbury Tales.* Guests at these hand-picked B & Bs rarely use alarm clocks. Instead, guests wake to pristine scents wafting to their rooms as deliciously distinct recipes are prepared. A joyous crescendo appears on cue as guests, new and repeat, comment on unique table appointments and well-polished silver. Veteran innkeepers featured in this cookbook break into self-satisfied smiles when flavor and menu design are praised. These celebrated innkeepers take time to nurture the conversation with as much care as their best sauce, so diners begin or end their day feeling physically and spiritually comforted.

This cookbook celebrates the joy of providing nourishment to sojourners along the way. Open its pages, smell its aroma, and bond with the men and women who provide you with the finest bed and breakfast experiences.

I want to congratulate M.J., my friend and mentor, on providing us with a '90s guide to the joy of healthy dining at the inn.

Julie Metcalf Cull, RD
Proprietor, Parson's Inn Bed and Breakfast

* * *
_____

Introduction

Of all the cookbooks I've written (there are nine others), this has the most "heart."

For in writing this book, I have come to know hundreds of innkeepers who love and protect their recipes like a freshly cleaned room before company arrives. I received calls and faxes and letters and e-mail from all over North America. The research phase of this project was as delightful as the holiday season, as the heart of the innkeeper oozed through the words and across the miles. I grew to recognize voices from Mississippi to Maine.

Where did the recipes come from? Some were from my travels. Other leads for low-fat recipes were passed along from friends who visit bed and breakfasts. I also wrote to well-known innkeeper-chefs and requested their favorites, and researched many B & B websites for healthy cuisine. I wanted a buffet of "all-American" dishes from Alaska and Hawaii to the tip of Florida, and over 40 states are represented.

As the recipes came in, I changed as little as possible. Most of the modifications were to reduce the fat content: I used lower-fat cheeses, skim milk, and liquid egg substitute, and I replaced some of the shortening in baked goods with nonfat sour cream or pureed fruit. Many of the recipes are in their original form, with innkeepers confessing they never tell guests they are dining "low fat" until the compliments come in.

I learned much about regional produce finding its way onto the breakfast table, like the Georgia Peach Breakfast Taco, and innkeepers' ingenious use of leftovers, like Banana Bonanza. I have smelled ethnic flavors coming from the kitchen, like Black Forest Coffeecake, Rojas Huevos Enchiladas, and Tepenade, and have grown to appreciate novel food ideas like Baked Grapefruit Alaska and Swiss Oatmeal.

History comes alive on these pages, as stories of Billy the Kid, General Hooker, Revolutionary War heroes, and the Cherokee Indians are shared from the parlors and sitting rooms.

This collection represents the best from the inns, and my expertise as a Registered Dietitian in keeping them healthy. The recipes are analyzed for calories, fat, and sodium. Exchange values are based on *The Exchange Lists for Meal Planning*, revised in 1995, by the American Dietetic Association and American Diabetes Association.

Some of the innkeepers shared their philosophy of service and personal mission statements. My favorite is from Jim and Renee Yeager from Romancing the Past Bed & Breakfast in Fulton, Missouri: "To offer hospitality using the gifts we have received, to serve others faithfully, administering God's grace." (I Peter 4:9–10).

* * *

Beverages

FRUIT SMOOTHIE DRINK
6 1-cup servings

1 banana
1 1/2 cups vanilla yogurt

6-ounce can frozen Welches mixed
fruit juice concentrate
1 tray ice cubes

1. Place all ingredients in blender. Add water to top. Blend on "liquefy" speed. Try as many combinations of fresh fruit and juice concentrates as you like, but always use a banana.

Calories per serving: 90 – Fat: 0 – Sodium: 29 mg.
For exchange diets, count: 1 1/2 fruit.
Preparation time: 5 minutes.

Used with permission of the innkeepers at Saltair Bed & Breakfast and Alpine Cottages

Saltair Bed & Breakfast and Alpine Cottages

Jan Bartlett & Nancy Saxton, Innkeepers
164 South 900 East
Salt Lake City, Utah 84102
(801) 533-8184; Toll free: (800) 733-8184;
Fax: (801) 595-0332
E-mail: saltair@travelase.com

Some houses have a welcome spirit or a familiar feeling about them, and Saltair Bed & Breakfast is one of those places. It is located in a wonderful Salt Lake City residential neighborhood with a tranquil atmosphere that complements the home. Guests are offered a choice of either a tasty full breakfast or a hearty continental fare. Saltair Bed & Breakfast is the oldest continuously running B & B in Utah, and once you experience the unique stay you will see why it has been around for so long.

FROZEN FRUIT SLUSH
12 3/4-cup servings

16-ounce can crushed pineapple
in juice
6-ounce can mandarin oranges
in juice
2 sliced bananas

1-pound bag frozen raspberries
6-ounce can orange juice concentrate
12-ounce can sugar-free Sprite
or similar soft drink

1. Stir all ingredients together in a large bowl, using juice from pineapples and oranges.

2. Ladle it into individual plastic party cups and freeze on trays for at least 4 hours. Remove cups as needed from freezer about 45 minutes

before serving time, enough time to soften, but not melt. Or thaw in the microwave by cooking on high power for 45 seconds.

3. Invert and serve in shallow china bowls with a sprig of fresh mint for garnish.

Calories per serving: 60 – Fat: 0 – Sodium: 15 mg.
For exchange diets, count: 1 fruit.
Preparation time: 20 minutes. – Freezing time: 4 hours.
Thawing time: 45 minutes or 45 seconds in microwave.

Used with permission of the innkeepers at Country Victorian B & B (see page 119)

TROPICAL FRUIT SMOOTHIES
8 3/4-cup servings

ice cubes
1/2 12-ounce can frozen guava nectar
1 cup pineapple juice

1 banana
1 cup fruit of your choice: mango, passionfruit, or strawberries

1. Select a blender or food processor that can chop ice cubes. Fill blender container one-third full of ice cubes.

2. Add frozen guava nectar and pineapple juice. Blend until smooth.

3. Add banana and blend again until smooth. Add other fruits for taste and color variety. Blend again until smooth, and serve in chilled stemmed glasses or parfait glasses.

4. For special touches, garnish with a sprig of mint or a fresh flower.

Calories per serving: 54 – Fat: 0 – Sodium: 2 mg.
For exchange diets, count 1 fruit.
Preparation time: 10 minutes.

Used with permission of the innkeeper at Poipu Bed & Breakfast Inn (see page 153)

Little Greenbrier Lodge Bed and Breakfast

Charles & Susan Lebon, Innkeepers
3685 Lyon Springs Road
Sevierville, Tennessee 37862
(423) 429-2500 (for information);
(800) 277-8100 (for reservations)

One of the oldest lodging facilities at the border of the Great Smoky Mountains National Park, the Little Greenbrier Lodge, built in 1939, is a bed and breakfast with Victorian elegance. For the hikers, this B & B is located right next to the park and just 150 yards from the Little Greenbrier trailhead.

TROPICAL LEMONADE

25 1-cup servings

12-ounce can frozen lemonade
2 6-ounce cans frozen orange juice
64-ounce can pineapple juice

1 gallon water
1 tablespoon vanilla extract
1 tablespoon almond extract

1. Combine all ingredients in large punch bowl or thermal cooler. Serve over crushed ice.

Calories per serving: 95 – Fat: 0 – Sodium: 3 mg.
For exchange diets, count: 1 1/2 fruit.
Preparation time: 10 minutes.

Used with permission of the innkeepers at Little Greenbrier Lodge Bed and Breakfast (see page 3)

ORANGE JULIUS

6 1-cup servings

6-ounce can frozen orange juice
1 cup skim milk
1/4 cup sugar

1 cup water
1 teaspoon vanilla
12 ice cubes

1. Place all ingredients in blender. Process until slushy.

Calories per serving: 100 – Fat: 0 – Sodium: 22 mg.
For exchange diets, count: 1 1/2 fruit.
Preparation time: 10 minutes.

Used with permission of the innkeepers at Four Columns Inn

Four Columns Inn

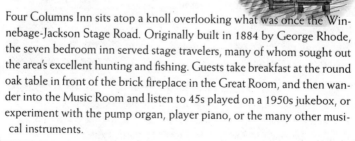

Norman & Pennie Kittleson, Innkeepers
Route 2, Box 75
(Exit 87 on I-90)
Sherburn, Minnesota 56171
(507) 764-8861

Four Columns Inn sits atop a knoll overlooking what was once the Winnebage-Jackson Stage Road. Originally built in 1884 by George Rhode, the seven bedroom inn served stage travelers, many of whom sought out the area's excellent hunting and fishing. Guests take breakfast at the round oak table in front of the brick fireplace in the Great Room, and then wander into the Music Room and listen to 45s played on a 1950s jukebox, or experiment with the pump organ, player piano, or the many other musical instruments.

Betty & Tony's Waterfront Bed & Breakfast

Betty & Tony Bridgens, Innkeepers
677 Broadview Avenue
Orillia, Ontario L3V 6P1
(705) 326-1125; Toll free: (800) 308-2579;
Fax: (705) 326-2262
E-mail: tony.bridgens@encode.com

A warm welcome awaits you at this beautiful waterfront home on Couchiching Point, a select residential area. Betty & Tony's Bed & Breakfast can accommodate you whether you come alone or with friends or children. In the morning, a full breakfast is served from the menu. Upon prior request, fresh homemade dinners can be served to you in the elegant dining room.

YE OLDE SOMERSET SCRUMPIE CIDER
A homemade sparkling fruit wine

125 5-ounce servings

13 48-ounce cans apple juice
(not from concentrate)
4 1/2 pounds sugar

wine yeast to cover the top of the juice
1/2 cup sugar

1. Pour apple juice into a sterile 5 gallon plastic pail with a lid.

2. Dissolve 4 1/2 pounds of sugar in the juice. Sprinkle wine yeast to cover the top of the liquid and stir, then leave in a warm place where fermentation can take place for 8 to 10 days, or until sediment settles out.

3. Siphon the liquid off the sediment and into a carboy; keep it cool till the cider is clear.

4. Siphon the cider back into the pail and dissolve 1/2 cup of sugar into it. Put the sweetened cider into sterile, pressure-resistant bottles, cap in a sterile way, and keep 2 to 4 weeks.

5. Treat as champagne when opening.

Calories per serving: 130 – Fat: 0 – Sodium: 5 mg.
For exchange diets, count: 2 fruit.
Preparation time: 20 minutes. – Fermentation time: 2 weeks.

Used with permission of the innkeepers at Betty & Tony's Waterfront Bed & Breakfast

Flemingsburg House Bed & Breakfast at Sweetwater Farm

Karin & Ray Bogardus, Innkeepers
3052 Old Murfreesboro Road
College Grove, Tennessee 37046
(615) 395-4247; Toll free: (800) 397-7092;
Fax: (615) 395-4243

The Flemingsburg House Bed & Breakfast is located midway between two historic Tennessee Civil War towns, Franklin and Murfreesboro, scenes of some of the fiercest fighting of the Civil War. The stately brick colonial structure was completed in 1830 by Josiah Fleming, one of Williamson County's earliest plantation owners. The house and "Big Hill" witnessed numerous skirmishes between Confederate defenders and the invading Yankee forces. Ray's Branch, a hillside spring, quenched the thirst of many Union soldiers. It is likely that the spring's value as a water source for the troops also saved the house from burning, which was the fate of so many neighboring structures. A country breakfast, complete with Karin's Austrian home fries and homemade breads is served.

HOT APPLE CIDER (HEISSER APPELWEIN)
16 1-cup servings

1 gallon apple wine or apple cider
1 large orange, slice thin and leave peels on
2 cinnamon sticks

5 cloves
1/2 lemon, slice thin and leave peel on
1/2 cup sugar, or to taste

1. Combine all ingredients in a 30-cup automatic coffee pot.

2. Let cider percolate until done.

Calories per serving: 143 – Fat: 0 – Sodium: 10 mg.
For exchange diets, count: 2 1/2 fruit.
Preparation time: 5 minutes. – Perking time: 20 minutes

Used with permission of the innkeepers at Flemingsburg House Bed & Breakfast at Sweetwater Farm

QUICK CAPPUCCINO FOR A CROWD
12 1-cup servings

12 cups water   14-ounce can evaporated skim milk
1 cup good quality regular grind coffee   3/4 cup sugar

1. Brew coffee in a 12-cup coffee maker using water and coffee.

2. While coffee is brewing, heat milk and sugar just to boiling in a saucepan.

3. Transfer milk and sugar mixture to an extra large thermal carafe. Pour in coffee.

Calories per serving: 57 – Fat: 0 – Sodium: 37 mg.
For exchange diets, count: 1 fruit.
Preparation time: 15 minutes.

Used with permission of the innkeeper at Abriendo Inn

Abriendo Inn

Kerrelyn M. Trent, Innkeeper
300 West Abriendo Avenue
Pueblo, Colorado 81004
(719) 544-2703; Fax: (719) 542-6544
E-mail: abriendo@rmi.net

The Abriendo Inn is a charming home with a red clay roof and white pillared facade framing a large, inviting veranda. Listed on the National Register of Historic Places, this is an inn where the elegance and style of an earlier era are readily apparent. You will feel like a treasured guest from the moment you walk through the front gate. Awake to a hearty breakfast served either in your room or in the lovely breakfast room downstairs. After breakfast you may enjoy strolling the grounds of the Abriendo or taking a leisurely walk through local neighborhoods and down historic Union Avenue. Then take off to the mountains where you'll find terrific hiking and biking trails as well as exhilarating rafting.

Appetizers

STRAWBERRIES AND DIP APPETIZER
4 1/2-cup servings

1 pint strawberries
1/4 cup nonfat sour cream

2 tablespoons brown sugar
Garnish: fresh mint

1. Select a large plate.

2. Arrange the berries in a wedge shape on one-third of the plate. Spoon the sour cream into a wedge shape covering another third of the plate, and spoon the sugar into the last wedge. Garnish the plate with fresh mint.

3. Dip berries into the sour cream, then into the brown sugar, and enjoy!

Calories per serving: 53 – Fat: 0 – Sodium: 21 mg.
For exchange diets, count: 1 fruit. – Preparation time: 5 minutes.

Used with permission of the innkeepers at Pineapple Hill Bed & Breakfast (see page 38)

TEPENADE
16 2-tablespoon servings

2–4 cloves fresh garlic (depending on your taste and size of clove), quartered
1 tablespoon extra virgin olive oil

2 tablespoons lemon juice
16-ounce can black olives
sea salt (preferably) to taste

1. Finely chop garlic by dropping into spinning food processor. Add olive oil. Scrape garlic off sides, then chop even finer. Add lemon juice and then black olives. Chop again, but not too finely. Salt to taste.

2. Spread on crisped rounds of French bread and serve.

Calories per serving: 76 – Fat: 7 g. – Sodium: 720 mg.
For exchange diets, count: 1 1/2 fat. – Preparation time: 10 minutes.

Used with permission of the innkeeper at Bienvenue House Bed & Breakfast

Bienvenue House Bed & Breakfast

Leslie Leonpacher, Innkeeper
421 North Main Street
St. Martinville, Louisiana 70582
(318) 394-9100; Toll free: (888) 394-9100;
Fax: (888) 394-9100
E-mail: bienvenu@iamerica.net

On the National Register of Historic Places, Bienvenue House has all the charm you would expect from a gracious southern 160-year-old home. In the heart of Cajun country, you will be welcomed to the bed and breakfast experience with this savory appetizer.

SMOKED SALMON PARFAIT
WITH PARMESAN TOAST

8 servings

16 ounces smoked salmon
8 ounces reduced-fat cream cheese, softened
3/4 cup evaporated skim milk
1/2 teaspoon white pepper, or to taste
1 medium red onion, chopped
1 cup chopped capers
1/2 cup chopped parsley
1 loaf French bread
1 cup freshly grated Parmesan cheese

1. Chill eight 8-ounce white wine glasses. In a food processor combine and puree salmon and cream cheese.

2. Slowly add evaporated milk until firm consistency. Add pepper.

3. Remove salmon mousse and put in pastry bag with open tip.

4. In each chilled glass layer 1 tablespoon onion, then approximately 2 ounces of the salmon mousse, 1 tablespoon capers, salmon mousse, 1/2 tablespoon parsley, and salmon mousse.

5. Preheat oven to 400°. Slice bread in thirds lengthwise and bake for five minutes. Sprinkle Parmesan cheese on each slice and bake again for another five minutes or until crisp. Slice and serve alongside parfait glass.

Calories per serving: 246 – Fat: 9 g. – Sodium: 826 mg.
For exchange diets, count: 2 lean meat, 1/2 skim milk, 1 starch.
Preparation time: 20 minutes.

Used with permission of the innkeepers at Kedron Valley Inn

Kedron Valley Inn

Max & Merrily Comins, Innkeepers
Route 106
South Woodstock, Vermont 05071
(802) 457-1473; Toll free: (800) 836-1193;
Fax: (802) 457-4469
E-mail: KedronInn@aol.com

One of Vermont's oldest inns, operating for over 168 years, the Kedron Valley Inn has been the setting for many romantic cotillions, weddings, and social extravaganzas where bedecked suitors whirled their ladies through contras and quadrilles. In the 1860s, it harbored fugitive slaves traveling the Underground Railroad to freedom. Today, the inn's rural pace and scenic surroundings nestled on 15 acres of rolling foothills of the Green Mountains offer a relaxing hideaway from the bustle of daily life. Contemporary American cuisine features fresh Vermont products.

Abigail's "Elegant Victorian Mansion"

Doug & Lily Vieyra, Innkeepers
1406 "C" Street
Eureka, California 95501
(707) 444-3144; Fax: (707) 442-5594

Located in the heart of California's rugged north
coast and giant redwood forests, a magic blend
of spectacular natural beauty, colorful history, Victorian architectural
wonders, and the roar of the Pacific Ocean all come together. This 1888
National Historic Landmark features a delicious multi-course French-
gourmet breakfast.

SMOKED SALMON MOUSSE
8 1/4-cup servings

1 teaspoon margarine
1 tablespoon finely chopped green
onions
3 ounces smoked salmon, boned
and flaked
1/4 cup 50% reduced-fat cream cheese

1/4 cup nonfat sour cream
2 tablespoons lemon juice
1 tablespoon vodka (optional)
1/4 cup nonfat whipped topping

1. Saute onions in margarine in a small skillet over medium heat until
golden.

2. Transfer to blender container; add salmon, cream cheese, and sour
cream, and blend well. Blend in lemon juice and vodka.

3. Transfer to a bowl and fold in whipped topping. Refrigerate at least
2 hours and then serve on crackers or warm French bread (see recipe
on page 72).

Calories per serving: 33 – Fat: 1 g. – Sodium: 121 mg.
For exchange diets, count: 1 very lean meat. – Preparation time: 15 minutes.
Chilling time: 2 hours.

Used with permission of the innkeepers at Abigail's "Elegant Victorian Mansion"

PESTO-CHEESE LOGS
12 3-tablespoon servings

1/4 cup walnuts
8 ounces reduced-fat cream cheese, softened
1/3 cup refrigerated pesto sauce
2 ounces feta cheese, crumbled

2 teaspoons cracked black pepper
2 tablespoons chopped fresh parsley
2 tablespoons finely shredded carrot
Garnish: carrot slivers, parsley, and fresh thyme

1. Preheat oven to 350°. Toast walnuts in a single layer on a baking sheet 8 to 10 minutes or until golden brown (stir frequently). Remove walnuts from sheet and cool.

2. Place walnuts in a food processor. Pulse until walnuts are ground, but not pasty. Remove from processor and set aside. Place cream cheese, pesto sauce, and feta cheese in food processor and process until smooth.

3. Spread 3/4 cup cheese mixture on a sheet of waxed paper and form a 4-inch-long log. Wrap waxed paper around the cheese mixture. Make a second log with remaining cheese mixture.

4. Refrigerate logs at least 4 hours. Roll each chilled log back and forth to form a 5-inch log. Combine walnuts and black pepper on one sheet of waxed paper. Unwrap one log and roll in nut mixture to coat. Combine parsley and carrot on another sheet of waxed paper. Unwrap the other log and roll in carrot mixture to coat. Serve immediately or wrap and refrigerate up to a day before serving. To serve, thinly slice logs and serve with crackers, breadsticks, or toasted bagel chips.

Calories per serving: 87 – Fat: 8 g. – Sodium: 159 mg.
For exchange diets, count: 2 fat. – Preparation time: 30 minutes.
Chilling time: at least 4 hours.

Used with permission of the innkeepers at Morning Star Inn

Morning Star Inn

**Pat & Pat Allen, Innkeepers
480 Flat Mountain Estates Road
Highlands, North Carolina 28741**

This jewel of an inn sits on Flat Mountain amid two acres of flowers and rock gardens at an elevation of 4,500 feet. Enjoy a delectable breakfast served in a southern gourmet style on our spacious sun porch offering a gorgeous view of Whiteside Mountain. Culinary delights may include southwestern eggs with chili peppers, spinach mushroom soufflé, Dr. Pat's famous cheese grits, or banana praline French toast. Chef/innkeeper Patricia Allen offers cooking classes for guests.

JALAPEÑO CHEESE BALL
12 1/4-cup servings

2 8-ounce packages cream cheese
1 teaspoon margarine
2 ounces blue cheese
1 tablespoon diced onion
1 tablespoon powdered onion
6 jalapeño peppers (remove all seeds),
   finely diced

juice of 1/2 lemon
1 tablespoon nonfat Miracle Whip
   salad dressing
dash salt
1/4 cup finely chopped pecans

1. Thoroughly combine all ingredients except pecans. Shape into ball and roll in crushed pecans. Refrigerate for at least 2 hours.

2. Serve with a selection of reduced-fat crackers.

Calories per serving: 119 – Fat: 10 g. – Sodium: 303 mg.
For exchange diets, count: 2 fat, 1/2 skim milk.
Preparation time: 10 minutes. Refrigeration time: 2 hours.

Used with permission of the innkeepers at Casa de Patron B and B Inn (see page 108)

DIP FOR FRUIT OR CHEESE
12 2-tablespoon servings

12-ounce carton 50% reduced-fat
   sour cream

3-ounce package sugar-free
   strawberry gelatin

1. Several hours before serving, combine sour cream and gelatin, stirring until smooth.

2. Chill for at least 2 hours. Serve as dip with chunks of fruit or cheese.

Calories per serving: 40 – Fat: 2 g. – Sodium: 30 mg.
For exchange diets, count: 1/2 skim milk.
Preparation time: 5 minutes. Chilling time: 2 hours.

Used with permission of the innkeepers at Down to Earth Lifestyles

Down to Earth Lifestyles

**Bill & Lola Coons, Innkeepers
12500 Northwest Crooked Road
Parkville, Missouri 64152
(816) 891-1018**

Down to Earth is a bed-and-breakfast experience for those who appreciate down-to-earth hospitality. The Coons have a beautiful earth-integrated home situated on 86 acres of peaceful woods and rolling hills. They are one of the few B & Bs that boasts of an indoor heated swimming pool. Or guests can stroll through the woods and over the pastures among the cattle, horses, and geese. People who like to fish will want to try their luck in the two stocked ponds.

CRABMEAT DIP
8 1/4-cup servings

1 garlic clove
1/4 teaspoon garlic powder
8-ounce package reduced-fat
   Philadelphia brand cream cheese
1/3 cup evaporated skim milk or
   nonfat sour cream

2 teaspoons lemon juice
2 teaspoons Worcestershire sauce
1 cup flaked crabmeat
dash of fresh ground pepper

1. Rub a mixing bowl with garlic clove that has been cut in half.

2. Place the garlic powder and cream cheese in the bowl and gradually add the milk to it. Mix until smooth and well blended. Add lemon juice, Worcestershire sauce, and crabmeat. Mix well. Season with pepper to taste.

3. Serve with reduced-fat potato chips or low-fat crackers.

Calories per serving: 82 – Fat: 5 g. – Sodium: 303 mg.
For exchange diets, count: 1/2 skim milk, 1 fat.
Preparation time: 10 minutes.

*Used with permission of the innkeepers at Stahlecker House Bed and Breakfast
Country Inn and Gardens*

Stahlecker House Bed and Breakfast Country Inn and Gardens

Ron & Ethel Stahlecker, Innkeepers
1042 Easum Drive
Napa Valley, California 94558
(707) 257-1588; Fax: (707) 224-7429
www.bnbweb.com/stahlecker.html

Secluded on 1 1/2 acres of manicured lawns, flowering gardens, and mature trees on a creek setting, the Stahlecker House B & B Country Inn is a nostalgic gem in Napa Valley. This inn was built in the late 1940s on the grounds of an existing apple orchard. Today, Stahlecker House is the beautifully decorated inn of vintage race car driver and pilot Ron and his local artist and wife Ethel Stahlecker. A chocolate chip cookie, coffee, and tea service commences each day at five in the evening. Tucked away on the relaxing sun deck in the 1929 antique icebox are iced tea and soft drinks for guests to enjoy at any time. A charming 1884 antique piano waits patiently for guests to entertain with tune. In the mornings, breakfast is by candlelight. Your hosts prepare a scrumptious full gourmet breakfast to tantalize the taste buds. Have your early morning coffee out on the patio or in the sun room.

The Tamworth Inn

Phil & Kathy Bender, Innkeepers
Main Street
Tamworth Village, New Hampshire 03886
(603) 323-7721;
Toll free: (800) NH2-RELAX (642-7352);
Fax: (603) 323-2026
E-mail: inn@tamworth.com

The Tamworth Inn is an authentic New England village inn located in the beautiful village of Tamworth, New Hampshire. The inn breakfast room serves a full country breakfast to inn guests and the public. The pub boasts a unique antique sled collection and offers a comfortable place for relaxation in front of a fire. A lighter fare menu is served in the pub. A quiet library with a fireplace has a wide selection of books and videos. There is a 20-foot by 40-foot swimming pool outside the pub's patio, and a large lawn leads to a gazebo, complete with hammock, on the bank of the sparkling Swift River at the rear of the inn.

ARTICHOKE APPETIZER
16 1/4-cup servings

8 ounces artichoke hearts
1 cup grated Parmesan cheese
1/2 cup nonfat sour cream
   or plain yogurt

1/2 cup nonfat mayonnaise
8 ounces reduced-fat cream cheese
2 garlic cloves, minced, or
   2 tablespoons chopped garlic

1. Preheat oven to 325°.

2. Place all ingredients in food processor and puree until smooth. Place in a 9- or 10-inch pie plate or decorative serving dish.

3. Bake for 30 to 40 minutes or until lightly browned on top. Serve with reduced-fat crackers, bread, or tortilla chips.

Calories per serving: 82 – Fat: 4 g. – Sodium: 297 mg.
For exchange diets, count: 1/2 skim milk, 1 fat.
Preparation time: 10 minutes. Baking time: 40 minutes.

Used with permission of the innkeepers at The Tamworth Inn

TORTILLA SWIRLS
12 2-swirl servings

8-ounce package reduced-fat cream cheese

4-ounce can chopped green chiles

chopped pimento, black olives, or radishes (optional)

3 flour tortillas

1. In a medium sized microwave-safe bowl, place cream cheese. Microwave for 30 to 40 seconds just to soften cheese; stir in chiles and mix well. Add chopped pimento, chopped radishes, and/or chopped black olives for color and pizzazz!

2. Spread mixture onto flat tortillas and roll jelly-roll style. Wrap rolled tortillas in plastic wrap and cool in refrigerator for about an hour. Remove and slice 1-inch thick. Serve as an appetizer on a plate with garnish.

Calories per serving: 43 – Fat: 1 g. – Sodium: 42 mg.
For exchange diets, count: 1/2 starch
Preparation time: 15 minutes – Chilling time: 1 hour

Used with permission of the innkeepers at Woodland Inn Bed & Breakfast

Woodland Inn Bed & Breakfast

Frank & Nancy O'Neil, Innkeepers
159 Trull Road
Woodland Park, Colorado 80863
(719) 687-8209; Toll free: (800) 226-9565;
Fax: (719) 687-3112

Relax in the homelike atmosphere of the Woodland Inn B & B, in the foothills of majestic Pikes Peak in the Colorado Rocky Mountains. A hearty breakfast is served in the dining room beside a warm fire or on the spacious patio. Refreshments are always available. This tasty snack is sent along as part of the field breakfast for the pilot and crew of the innkeepers' hot air balloon, High Time. Guests may join the festivities through the "crew package" special.

SPINACH POM POMS
12 servings, 3 pom poms each

nonstick cooking spray
10-ounce package frozen chopped
  spinach, drained and squeezed dry
1 cup herb-seasoned stuffing mix,
  crushed fine

1/2 cup grated Parmesan cheese
3 eggs, well beaten, or 3/4 cup liquid
  egg substitute
1/4 cup reduced-fat margarine
dash nutmeg

1. Preheat oven to 350°.

2. Spray a baking sheet with nonstick cooking spray.

3. Combine all ingredients in a mixing bowl.

4. Shape mixture into walnut-size pieces and place on baking sheet. Bake for 12 to 15 minutes or until browned. Serve with sweet and spicy mustard (see recipe page 179).

Note: These appetizers can be prepared and frozen before baking. Place pom poms on a cookie sheet and freeze. Then transfer to plastic freezer bags for storage. Remove from freezer and bake for 15 minutes or until golden brown.

Calories per serving: 73 – Fat: 4 g. – Sodium: 224 mg.
For exchange diets, count: 1 vegetable, 1 fat.
Preparation time: 15 minutes. – Baking time: 15 minutes.

Used with permission of the innkeepers at The Chestnut House Bed & Breakfast

The Chestnut House Bed & Breakfast

Frank & Elizabeth Caré, Innkeepers
1911 Lakeshore Drive
St. Joseph, Michigan 49085
(616) 983-7413; Fax: (616) 983-2122

At the Chestnut House, the gourmet breakfast is a special treat. In British tradition you'll enjoy homemade scones and muffins and breakfast entrées that often include fresh herbs from Elizabeth's garden, served to you on English china in a cheery solarium that overlooks Lake Michigan. In the evening you will be greeted with scrumptious hors d'oeuvres served by a warming fireplace when it's chilly. In warmer weather, the decks surrounding the pool often become the site for these delicious tidbits.

SWEET & SOUR MEATBALLS
8 3-meatball servings

3 slices bread, diced
1/2 cup water
1 pound ground beef
1 cup dry milk
1/4 cup minced onion
1 egg or 1/4 cup liquid egg substitute

1/4 teaspoon seasoned salt
1/4 teaspoon seasoned pepper
1 can tomato soup
1/2 cup brown sugar
2 tablespoons vinegar
1 teaspoon dry mustard

1. Preheat oven to 375°.

2. Mix first eight ingredients and form into 24 small meatballs. Place in baking pan and bake for 30 minutes. Pour off all fat.

3. Combine remaining ingredients in a bowl and pour the sauce over meatballs. Bake for at least a half hour, basting with sauce occasionally.

Calories per serving: 247 – Fat: 8 g. – Sodium: 530 mg.
For exchange diets, count: 2 lean meat, 1 fruit, 1 starch.
Preparation time: 15 minutes. Baking time: 1 hour.

Used with permission of the innkeepers at The Oliver Inn B & B (see page 142)

PUFFED CRAB ROLL
8 servings

nonstick cooking spray
1/4 cup margarine
3/4 cup all-purpose flour
1/4 teaspoon salt
1/4 teaspoon ground nutmeg
2 cups skim milk
6 eggs or 1 1/2 cups liquid egg
   substitute
1 tablespoon margarine

2 tablespoons all-purpose flour
dash of salt
dash Tabasco sauce
1 1/3 cups evaporated skim milk
2 tablespoons sherry
2 cups coarsely flaked imitation
   crabmeat
Garnish: red cocktail sauce

1. Spray a 15 x 10 x 1-inch baking pan with nonstick cooking spray. Preheat the oven to 400°.

2. In a heavy medium saucepan, melt 1/4 cup margarine. Stir in the 3/4 cup flour, 1/4 teaspoon salt, and nutmeg. Add milk. Cook and stir over medium heat until mixture follows the spoon around the saucepan.

3. Remove from heat and cool for 5 minutes. Add eggs or egg substitute, beating with a wire whisk until combined.

4. Spread egg mixture into the prepared baking pan. Bake for 20 to 25 minutes or until the omelet is puffy and golden.

5. Meanwhile, melt 1 tablespoon margarine in a heavy saucepan. Stir in the 2 tablespoons flour, dash salt, and Tabasco sauce. Add evaporated milk all at once. Cook and stir until thickened and bubbly. Add

sherry, then cook and stir for one minute more. Stir in the crabmeat. Cook just till heated through. Set filling aside.

6. Line a flat surface with a large sheet of waxed paper. When the omelet is done, immediately loosen it from the pan and invert the omelet onto the sheet of waxed paper. Spread omelet with filling. Roll up omelet without the waxed paper, jelly-roll style, starting from the short sides. Transfer crab roll to a serving platter, cut, and serve with red cocktail sauce.

Calories per serving: 205 – Fat: 9 g. – Sodium: 578 mg.
For exchange diets, count: 2 lean meat, 1 starch, 1/2 fat.
Preparation time: 20 minutes. – Baking time: 25 minutes.

Used with permission of the innkeepers at Inn at Poplar Corner (see page 148)

Chalet Kilauea—The Inn at Volcano

Lisha & Brian Crawford, Innkeepers
Wright Road
P.O. Box 998
Volcano Village, Hawaii 96785
(808) 967-7786;
Toll free: (800) 937-7786;
Fax: (808) 577-1849
E-mail: bchawaii@aol.com

Explore treasures from around the world at Chalet Kilauea. Brian and Lisha Crawford, the consummate hosts at this inn, are international travelers who know the art of hospitality. The candlelit gourmet breakfasts are served on fine china with linen and crystal in an elegant dining room with black and white tile floors and French windows looking out onto a flower-fringed lawn. A light supper is also served.

HAWAIIAN-STYLE CROUTE FROMAGE
1 serving

1 thick slice Hawaiian Portuguese
  sweet bread
1 teaspoon nonfat mayonnaise
1/8 cup shredded reduced-fat
  cheddar cheese
1/8 cup shredded reduced-fat Monterey
  Jack cheese

1 slice fresh tomato
1 teaspoon chopped macadamia nut
3 slivers green onion
1 tablespoon sweet guava Thai chile
  sauce (optional)

1. Lightly toast or grill bread on both sides.

2. Spread with mayonnaise and place in shallow casserole dish. Cover with both cheeses, and put under broiler until melted, but not browned.

3. Add tomato slice, and return to broiler until browned.

4. Garnish with macadamia nuts and green onion. Add chile sauce if desired.

Calories per serving: 155 – Fat: 6 g. – Sodium: 405 mg.
For exchange diets, count: 1 1/2 starch, 1 lean meat.
Preparation time: 10 minutes.

Used with permission of the innkeepers at Chalet Kilauea—The Inn at Volcano (see page 20)

CRAB PUFFS
96 puffs or 12 servings, 8 puffs each

6-ounce can crabmeat
5-ounce jar Kraft Old English cheese
  spread
2 tablespoons soft margarine

2 tablespoons nonfat mayonnaise
1/2 teaspoon garlic salt
1/2 teaspoon seasoned salt
6 English muffins

1. Combine all ingredients except English muffins in a mixing bowl and use an electric mixer to mix well.

2. Split muffins into halves and spread mixture equally onto each half.

3. Cut halves into eighths. Place 3 inches under broiler until cheese melts. Keep the oven door slightly open and watch carefully to avoid burning. Broiling will take 4 to 6 minutes.

Calories per serving (8 puffs): 199 – Fat: 5 g. – Sodium: 714 mg.
For exchange diets, count: 1 very lean meat, 2 starch.
Preparation time: 15 minutes. – Broiling time: 5 minutes.

Used with permission of the innkeepers at The Chestnut House Bed & Breakfast (see page 18)

BAKED BRIE IN A BREAD BOWL
16 servings

1 teaspoon unsalted margarine
1/2 cup nonfat sour cream
1/2 tablespoon minced garlic
8 ounces Brie, rind trimmed, cut into chunks
8 ounces reduced-fat cream cheese, cut into pieces
1 small onion, chopped (about 3/4 cup)

2 teaspoons lemon juice
2 teaspoons brown sugar
1/2 teaspoon Worcestershire sauce
salt and pepper to taste
8-ounce round sourdough or peasant loaf
paprika

1. Melt margarine in medium skillet over medium to low heat. Add onion and sauté about 5 minutes, then add garlic. Sauté until onion is golden brown (about 5 more minutes). Set aside.

2. Place Brie and cream cheese in a large microwave-safe bowl. Microwave on medium until just melted (about 2 to 3 minutes). Whisk onion mixture, sour cream, lemon juice, brown sugar, and Worcestershire sauce into melted cheese mixture. Season to taste with salt and pepper.

3. Cut off top of bread loaf (in the same manner as if carving a pumpkin). Scoop out interior of loaf, leaving 3/4-inch shell of bread. Spoon cheese mixture into loaf; replace bread lid. Wrap in foil.

4. Preheat oven to 400°. Bake loaf until filling bubbles, about 30 to 45 minutes. Unwrap and place on platter; remove bread lid. Sprinkle with paprika. Serve with assorted crudites or chunks of Italian or French bread. This can be prepared one day ahead and refrigerated and baked before serving. Let stand at room temperature 10 minutes before serving.

Calories per serving: 187 – Fat: 8 g. – Sodium: 303 mg.
For exchange diets, count: 1 lean meat, 1 starch, 1 fat.
(Nutrition analysis does not include bread cubes or crudités.)
Preparation time: 15 minutes. Baking time: 45 minutes. Standing time: 10 minutes.

Used with permission of the innkeepers at Fitch Hill Inn Bed & Breakfast

APPETIZER PIZZA

4 servings

2 medium pita breads (about 6 inches)   2 sliced tomatoes
4 minced garlic cloves   1/2 cup shredded mozzarella cheese
bunch of fresh basil   2 teaspoons extra virgin olive oil

1. Preheat oven to 400°.

2. Separate each pita into two. Put pita bread on cookie sheets. Spread 1 minced garlic clove onto each pita round. Arrange 4-6 basil leaves over garlic. Top with 3 slices of tomato. Sprinkle about 2 tablespoons of shredded cheese on each and drizzle with olive oil.

3. Bake for about 15 minutes or until cheese melts and pizzas are bubbly. Serve as whole pizza immediately.

Calories per serving: 151 – Fat: 5 g. – Sodium: 186 mg.
For exchange diets, count: 1 starch, 1 vegetable, 1 fat.
Preparation time: 10 minutes. Baking time: 15 minutes.

Used with permission of the innkeepers at The Combes Family Inn (see page 120)

Fitch Hill Inn Bed & Breakfast

Richard Pugliese & Stanley Corklin, Innkeepers
258 Fitch Hill Road
Hyde Park, Vermont, 05655
(802) 888-3834; Toll free: (800) 639-2903;
Fax: (802) 888-7789

Come to the Fitch Hill Inn and discover a taste of the past in a history filled home, built circa 1797 in Hyde Park, Vermont. The home was built by Darius Fitch, son of Jabez Fitch, one of the founders of Hyde Park and a Captain in the Revolutionary force during the U.S. War of Independence. The home has served as part of a working farm, been used as a schoolhouse, and has been a country inn for over a decade. Breakfast and dinner are special events. A typical breakfast includes fresh ground Green Mountain Coffee, fresh fruit juices, fresh fruit, hot or cold cereals, and a main course of raspberry cream-filled French toast or blueberry pancakes served with Vermont maple syrup.

Marie's Bed and Breakfast

Roy & Marie Werkmeister, Innkeepers
969 - 7th Street
P. O. Box 812
Lake View, Iowa 51450
(712) 657-2486

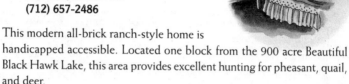

This modern all-brick ranch-style home is handicapped accessible. Located one block from the 900 acre Beautiful Black Hawk Lake, this area provides excellent hunting for pheasant, quail, and deer.

MICROWAVE CARAMEL CORN
12 2-cup servings

6 quarts air-popped corn	1/3 cup light corn syrup
1 cup brown sugar	1/2 teaspoon salt
1/4 cup soft margarine	1/2 teaspoon soda

1. Prepare popcorn and transfer to a heavy, clean brown paper bag.

2. Mix brown sugar, margarine, corn syrup, and salt in a deep microwave-safe mixing bowl. Microwave on high power for 2 minutes. Stir and then microwave another 2 minutes. Then stir in soda.

3. Pour syrup over popcorn and shake. Microwave the bag on high power for 1 1/2 minutes. Shake the bag and microwave another 1 1/2 minutes. Pour caramel corn on a baking sheet to cool. Store in an airtight container.

Calories per serving: 131 – Fat: 3 g. – Sodium: 185 mg.
For exchange diets, count: 1 1/2 starch.
Preparation time: 20 minutes.

Used with permission of the innkeepers at Marie's Bed and Breakfast

HARVEST POPCORN
12 1-cup servings

2 quarts air-popped popcorn, unsalted
3-ounce package shoestring potatoes
  or 3 ounces pretzel nuggets
1/2 cup reduced-fat mixed nuts
  or peanuts
2 tablespoons soft margarine, melted

1 teaspoon dried dillweed
1 teaspoon Worcestershire sauce
1/2 teaspoon lemon pepper
1/2 teaspoon garlic powder
1/2 teaspoon onion powder

1. Preheat oven to 325°.

2. In large roasting pan, mix popcorn, potatoes, and nuts.

3. In a small saucepan, combine margarine and remaining ingredients. Pour over popcorn mixture; stir until well coated.

4. Bake for 8 to 10 minutes, stirring once. Cool. Store in tightly covered containers. Great for snacks or for gifts.

Calories per serving: 80 – Fat: 5 g. – Sodium: 57 mg.
For exchange diets, count: 1 starch.
Preparation time: 15 minutes. Baking time: 10 minutes.

Used with permission of the innkeepers at Wilkum Inn B & B

Wilkum Inn B & B

Annamae Chambers & Barbara Jones, Innkeepers
P.O. Box 1115
Idyllwild, California 92549-1115
(909) 659-4087; Toll free: (800) 659-4086

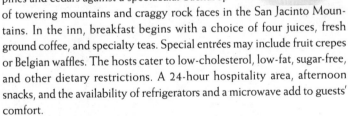

This two-story, shingle-style inn nestles among pines and cedars against a spectacular backdrop of towering mountains and craggy rock faces in the San Jacinto Mountains. In the inn, breakfast begins with a choice of four juices, fresh ground coffee, and specialty teas. Special entrées may include fruit crepes or Belgian waffles. The hosts cater to low-cholesterol, low-fat, sugar-free, and other dietary restrictions. A 24-hour hospitality area, afternoon snacks, and the availability of refrigerators and a microwave add to guests' comfort.

* * *

Fruits

ANNIE'S FRUIT DIP
8 1/2-cup servings

3 ounces fat-free cream cheese
7 ounces marshmallow creme
1/4 teaspoon lemon extract
2 drops red food coloring

4 cups prepared fresh fruits for
dipping, such as pears, apples,
oranges, grapes, and bananas

1. Place cream cheese and marshmallow creme in a 1 1/2-quart bowl. Microwave on 50 percent power for 2 minutes. Stir. Repeat cooking and stir until smooth. Fold in lemon extract and food coloring and transfer to a serving bowl. May refrigerate until serving.

2. Prepare assorted fresh fruits for dipping. (See recipe for Portrait of Fruit, page 31.) Soak bananas, apples, and pears in chilled orange juice to prevent browning. Provide toothpicks for fruit dippers.

Calories per serving: 154 – Fat: 1 g. – Sodium: 31 mg.
For exchange diets, count: 2 1/2 fruit. – Preparation time: 10 minutes.

Used with permission of the innkeepers at Parson's Inn Bed and Breakfast

---

Parson's Inn Bed & Breakfast

Julie Metcalf Cull & Mary Huser, Innkeepers
Rock School Road
P.O. Box 67
Glen Haven, WI 53810
(608) 794-2491

The Parson's Inn is a distinctive three-story red brick house that was once the home of Catholic priests serving this Mississippi River community in rural southwestern Wisconsin. The home is surrounded by a wraparound white porch and ever-blooming perennials and fresh herbs. Julie is a successful cookbook author and registered dietitian, and a sought-after speaker at both bed-and-breakfast and professional nutrition meetings throughout the United States. Mary tends to her guests and cooking with care.

FRESH FRUIT 'N HONEY
8 3/4-cup servings

3/4 cup nonfat mayonnaise
1/2 cup honey
1 tablespoon fresh lemon juice
1/2 teaspoon almond extract

8 ounces sugar-free nonfat vanilla
yogurt
4 cups chunked fresh fruit of the
season

1. Mix mayonnaise, honey, lemon juice, and almond extract with a spoon. Fold in yogurt. Cover and refrigerate until serving time.

2. Serve 1/4 cup dressing over 1/2 cup chunked fresh fruit in fruit dishes.

Calories per serving: 138 – Fat: 0 – Sodium: 312 mg.
For exchange diets, count: 1 1/2 fruit, 1/2 skim milk.
Preparation time: 10 minutes. Chilling time: 30 minutes

Used with permission of the innkeepers at King's Inn at Georgetown Bed & Breakfast

FROSTY ORANGE CUP
20 servings

10 large oranges
2 16-ounce cans apricot halves with juice, chopped
10 1/2-ounce can pineapple tidbits with juice
3 bananas, sliced

1 cup flaked coconut
1/2 cup sugar
6-ounce can frozen orange juice concentrate, thawed
1 tablespoon fresh lemon juice

1. Cut each orange in half in a saw-tooth pattern. Remove orange sections and reserve. Clip membranes inside orange shells and remove.

2. Place orange shells in freezer until thoroughly chilled.

3. Combine orange sections with remaining ingredients and mix thoroughly.

4. Spoon mixture into prepared orange shells. Return to freezer for at least 3 hours. Remove from freezer 30 minutes before serving. Extra orange mixture may be frozen in muffin tins lined with paper baking cups.

Calories per serving: 116 – Fat: 1 g. – Sodium: 23 mg.
For exchange diets, count: 2 fruit. – Preparation time: 20 minutes.
Freezing time: 3 1/2 hours. Standing time: 30 minutes.

Used with permission of the innkeepers at King's Inn at Georgetown Bed & Breakfast

King's Inn at Georgetown Bed & Breakfast

Marilyn & Jerry Burkhardt, Innkeepers
230 Broad Street
Georgetown, South Carolina 29440
(803) 527-6937; (800) 251-8805;
Fax: (803) 527-6937

The Southern tradition of this mansion dating to 1825 is evident in the abundance of heirlooms, antiques, and reproduction period pieces that fill the inn. This one-of-a kind getaway has a lap pool and a croquet lawn. There are walking and jitney tours of the historic district and boat tours of the plantations nearby.

HOMEMADE HIGH-CALCIUM NONFAT YOGURT
4 1-cup servings

2 cups nonfat powdered milk
1 teaspoon live yogurt culture

3 cups 98° (body temperature) tap
water

1. Put powdered milk in a 1 1/2- or 2-quart glass container. Add yogurt
culture, and slowly pour in tap water, mixing thoroughly.

2. Cover tightly with plastic wrap and place container in a small cooler.
Fill the container with 140° tap water up to the neck of the quart measure. Close cooler and allow yogurt to thicken for 8 hours in a warm
place. Refrigerate.

Calories per serving: 217 – Fat: 0 – Sodium: 321 mg.
For exchange diets, count: 2 1/2 skim milk. – Calcium: 754 mg.
Preparation time: 5 minutes. Incubation time: 8 hours.

Used with permission of the innkeepers at Country Homestead Bed and Breakfast

MARINATED FRUIT
12 1/2-cup servings

20-ounce can sweetened pineapple
chunks
2 pears cut into chunks
2 apples cut into chunks
2 peaches cut into chunks (frozen peach
slices may be substituted)

2 tablespoons orange juice
concentrate
1 teaspoon honey
1 teaspoon chopped fresh mint

1. Drain pineapple and reserve juice. Combine fruit and set aside.

2. Combine reserved pineapple juice, orange juice concentrate, honey,
and mint; pour over fruit and toss gently. Cover and chill until serving.

Calories per serving: 73 – Fat: 0 – Sodium: 2 mg.
For exchange diets, count: 1 fruit. – Preparation time: 15 minutes.
Chilling time: 30minutes

Used with permission of the innkeepers at The Schell Haus Bed & Breakfast (see page 87)

PORTRAIT OF FRUIT
10 1-cup servings

1 bunch leafy lettuce
1 pineapple
1 pound red grapes
3 bananas, sliced into 1-inch chunks

2 kiwifruit, peeled and sliced
2 red apples, sliced and dipped in
orange juice

1. Line an oval fruit platter with lettuce. Cut the top off the pineapple and place the top at one end of the platter. Cut the body of the pineapple in two lengthwise. Using a paring knife, cut out the fresh pineapple, removing the fibrous spikes and center.

2. Cube pineapple and decorate the two empty pineapple shells with all the fruits, creating your own "portrait" on the platter.

Calories per serving: 101 – Fat: 0 – Sodium: 2 mg.
For exchange diets, count: 2 fruit. – Preparation time: 20 minutes.

Used with permission of the innkeepers at Parson's Inn Bed and Breakfast (see page 28)

SUNSHINE FRUIT BOWL
8 3/4-cup servings

1 pint fresh strawberries, cleaned,
stemmed, and sliced
2 fresh peaches, peeled and sliced

2 bananas, sliced
1/4 cup blueberries
2 tablespoons orange juice concentrate

1. In a large bowl, combine fruits.

2. Drizzle orange juice concentrate on top and stir gently.

Calories per serving: 80 – Fat: 0 – Sodium: 7 mg.
For exchange diets, count: 1 1/2 fruit. – Preparation time: 15 minutes.

Used with permission of the innkeepers at Eagles' Landing Bed and Breakfast (see page 52)

YOGURT FRUIT PARFAIT
4 servings

1 cup date-nut granola or your
favorite granola
2 cups plain, lemon chiffon, or vanilla
nonfat yogurt

2 bananas, sliced
2 cups sliced strawberries or any
other berries

1. Spoon half of the granola into 4 parfait glasses. Top with half of the yogurt, followed by the banana slices, and then spread the berries on the banana, saving a few berries for garnish.

2. Top with remaining granola and yogurt. Garnish with berries on top.

Calories per serving: 200 – Fat: 2 g. – Sodium: 90 mg.
For exchange diets, count: 1 fruit, 1 skim milk, 1/2 starch.
Preparation time: 10 minutes.

Used with permission of the innkeepers at Forget-Me-Not Bed & Breakfast (see page 59)

STRAWBERRY COMPOTE
16 1/4-cup servings

2 cups diced rhubarb
2 cups quartered strawberries
1 cup sugar

1 vanilla bean
1 tablespoon coarsely chopped
ginger

1. Place the fruit and sugar in a medium-size saucepan over medium heat. Cook till tender, 8 to 10 minutes. Add vanilla bean and ginger. Serve warm or cool on your favorite waffles, pancakes, or French toast.

Calories per serving: 57 – Fat: 0 – Sodium: 1 mg.
For exchange diets, count: 1 fruit. – Preparation time: 10 minutes.
Cooking time: 10 minutes.

Used with permission of the innkeepers at Palisades Bed & Breakfast at Dash Point

Palisades Bed & Breakfast at Dash Point

Dennis & Peggy LaPorte, Innkeepers
5162 SW 311th Place
Federal Way, Washington 98023
(253) 838-4376;
Toll free: (888) 838-4376;
Fax: (253) 838-1480
E-mail: laporte2@ix.netcom.com

This unique waterfront property in Dash Point overlooks Puget Sound with incredible views of the Olympic Mountains and breathtaking sunsets. This bed and breakfast is designed to offer a luxurious getaway in very private, serene, and comfortable surroundings. Upon entering this home, guests are offered a beverage of choice, with fruit and cheese in the pine-paneled living room with fireplace; while a grand player-piano fills the air with favorite melodies.

1790 House—Bed & Breakfast Inn

Patricia & John Wiley, Innkeepers
630 Highmarket Street
Georgetown, South Carolina 29440
(803) 546-4821; Toll free: (800) 890-7432

Among South Carolina's finest residences, the 1790 House is historically and architecturally significant. This meticulously restored 200-year-old West Indies colonial plantation-style inn is located within the heart of the Georgetown National Register Historic District. Guests may enjoy gourmet breakfasts served on the veranda or in the dining room. Juice, fresh fruit, homemade muffins, and breads accompany specialties from the kitchen, along with fine teas and coffees.

AMARETTO GLAZED FRUIT
12 3/4-cup servings

2 16-ounce cans pear halves, reserve juice
1 teaspoon cornstarch
2 tablespoons amaretto
2 teaspoons brown sugar
1/2 teaspoon vanilla

nonstick cooking spray
16-ounce can apricot halves, drained
1 can pineapple chunks, drained
Garnish: frozen vanilla yogurt and/or finely chopped nuts

1. In small bowl combine 1/3 cup of reserved pear juice with the cornstarch and stir until blended. Then add amaretto, brown sugar, and vanilla. Stir well. Set aside.

2. Spray a large skillet with cooking spray. Add pear halves, apricot halves, and pineapple chunks to warmed pan, and saute for 2 to 3 minutes.

3. Pour in amaretto mixture and cook over medium heat for a few minutes until thickened, stirring frequently. Do not overcook.

4. Place in individual serving dishes or you may use this as a warm side dish with a hot entree. Top with a dollop of yogurt and/or sprinkle with finely chopped nuts.

Calories per serving: 74 – Fat: 0 – Sodium: 4 mg.
For exchange diets, count: 1 fruit. – Preparation time: 15 minutes.

Used with permission of the innkeepers at 1790 House—Bed & Breakfast Inn

BAKED FRUIT COMPOTE

12 2/3-cup servings

16 ounces pitted sweet dark cherries in juice
1/4 cup firmly packed brown sugar
1 tablespoon cornstarch
2 tablespoons lemon juice
1/4 cup orange juice

29-ounce can sliced peaches in juice, drained and juice reserved
6 ounces dried apricots
6 ounces pitted prunes
1 tablespoon cherry brandy

1. Preheat oven to 350°.

2. Drain cherries thoroughly and reserve liquid.

3. In a medium mixing bowl, combine brown sugar and cornstarch. Gradually stir in cherry juice, lemon juice, and orange juice.

4. In a 2-quart casserole, combine cherries, peaches, apricots, and prunes. Pour brown sugar and juice mixture over the fruit. Sprinkle with cherry brandy.

5. Cover and bake for 45 minutes or until the apricots are tender. Serve warm.

Calories per serving: 123 – Fat: 0 – Sodium: 8 mg.
For exchange diets, count: 2 fruit. – Preparation time: 15 minutes.
Baking time: 45 minutes.

Used with permission of the innkeepers at Bauer Haus Bed & Breakfast

Bauer Haus Bed & Breakfast

Marian & Dick Bauer, Innkeepers
362 North College Street (U.S. 127)
Harrodsburg, Kentucky 40330
(606) 734-6289

This 1880s Victorian inn, located in Kentucky's oldest settlement, is listed on the National Register of Historic Places and designated a Kentucky Landmark. Downstairs are the large main entry hall, parlor, sitting room, dining room, kitchen, and the Bauer's living quarters. Guests use the front stairway that leads to four large guest rooms on the second floor. There is a third-floor ballroom that is not yet open to guests and a newly constructed carriage house at the back of the property that will have an additional upstairs guest room.

BAKED PEARS
8 servings

nonstick cooking spray
4 pears, halved, peeled, and cored
1/4 teaspoon cinnamon
1/8 teaspoon nutmeg
2 tablespoons reduced-fat butter-
  flavored margarine

1/4 cup brown sugar
Garnish: nonfat whipped topping or
  fat-free vanilla yogurt

1. Preheat oven to 350°.

2. Spray a pie plate with cooking spray.

3. Place the pear halves in the prepared pie plate, arranged like spokes with narrow ends pointed toward the center. Sprinkle the pears with the cinnamon and nutmeg. Cover and set aside.

4. In a small bowl, combine the margarine and brown sugar thoroughly, and then carefully spread the mixture over the pears.

5. Bake for 20 to 25 minutes. Serve warm. Top with whipped topping or yogurt if you like.

Calories per serving: 74 – Fat: 2 g. – Sodium: 19 mg.
For exchange diets, count: 1 fruit, 1/2 fat. – Preparation time: 10 minutes.
Baking time: 20 minutes.

Used with permission of the innkeeper at Rocking Horse Manor Bed & Breakfast

Rocking Horse Manor Bed & Breakfast

Diana Jachumiak, Innkeeper
1022 South 3rd Street
Louisville, Kentucky 40203
(502) 583-0408; 1-888-HORSE-BB;
Fax: (502) 583-6077 ext. 129

This Richardsonian Romanesque mansion built in 1888 combines old-world charm with modern amenities in each of its five guest rooms. A full gourmet breakfast, served in the dining room, offers an assortment of muffins, quiches, breads, and fresh fruits. And it is conveniently located near Churchill Downs.

POACHED PEARS IN RASPBERRY SAUCE
4 servings

4 Bosc pears
1/4 cup maple syrup
cinnamon and brown sugar to taste

16-ounce package frozen whole
raspberries or fresh in season
sugar to taste

1. Peel pears and cut off bottom, so pears will stand up straight. Place in microwave dish.

2. Spoon 1 tablespoon of maple syrup over each pear. Sprinkle each pear with cinnamon and brown sugar. Cover dish completely with plastic wrap. Cook in microwave on high for 10 or 12 minutes or until pears are tender, but not too soft.

3. Meanwhile, heat berries in a small saucepan over medium heat to a simmer, saving a few berries for garnish.

4. Remove berries and transfer to a blender; puree until smooth.

5. Place a strainer or sieve over a bowl, and pour berries through to remove seeds. Add sugar as desired.

6. To serve: place poached pears on serving plate and cover with sauce or put sauce on plate and set pears in the center. Garnish with a few whole berries.

Calories per serving: 180 – Fat: 1 g. – Sodium: 4 mg.
For exchange diets, count: 3 fruit. – Preparation time: 20 minutes.

Used with permission of the innkeepers at Abigail's "Elegant Victorian Mansion" (see page 12)

BAKED GRAPEFRUIT ALASKA
4 servings

2 egg whites
1/4 teaspoon cream of tartar
3 tablespoons sugar
1/4 cup orange marmalade

2 grapefruit, cut in half and scored
1-2 tablespoons coconut flakes
Garnish: 4 fresh mint sprigs

1. Preheat oven to 350°.

2. Beat egg whites and cream of tartar till fluffy and stiff; add sugar slowly while beating. Keep beating until peaks are very stiff and you can turn bowl upside down without the mixture falling out.

3. Carefully fold in orange marmalade. Heap on top of grapefruit halves and sprinkle with coconut flakes.

4. Bake on greased sheet for 5–8 minutes or until brown. Garnish with mint.

Calories per serving: 131 – Fat: 1 g. – Sodium: 14 mg.
For exchange diets, count: 2 fruit. – Preparation time: 15 minutes.
Baking time: 8 minutes.

Used with permission of the innkeepers at Stitt House Bed & Breakfast Inn

Stitt House Bed & Breakfast Inn

Horst & Linda Fischer, Innkeepers
824 Park Avenue
Hot Springs National Park, Arkansas 71901
Phone & Fax: (501) 623-2704
E-mail: stittbb@hsnp.com

The Stitt house, listed on the National Register of Historic Places, was built in 1875 by Samuel H. Stitt, one of the city's most prominent and industrious early businessmen, and is said to be the oldest dwelling still standing in Hot Springs. Because it remained in the Stitt family until 1983, when the Fischers purchased the property, the mansion remains very much as it was originally built. Linda used to own a nationally-recognized gourmet restaurant for many years and shares her talent with the guests. The owners take pride in having been featured in *Fodor's America's Best Bed and Breakfast* and were also featured on the television program *Country Inn USA*.

BAKED PINEAPPLE
6 1/2-cup servings

nonstick cooking spray
2 tablespoons cornstarch
1/4 cup water
2 eggs beaten or 1/2 cup liquid egg substitute
15 1/4-ounce can crushed pineapple, undrained
1/2 cup sugar
1 teaspoon vanilla extract
1 tablespoon butter-flavored margarine
ground cinnamon

1. Preheat oven to 350°.

2. Spray a 1 1/2-quart baking dish with cooking spray.

3. Combine cornstarch and water in a mixing bowl; stir until smooth. Add eggs, and blend well. Add pineapple, sugar, and vanilla; mix well.

4. Pour into prepared baking dish; dot with margarine, and sprinkle with cinnamon. Bake for 1 hour.

Calories per serving: 171 – Fat: 2 g. – Sodium: 61 mg.
For exchange diets, count: 2 1/2 fruit, 1/2 fat. – Preparation time: 15 minutes.
Baking time: 1 hour.

Used with permission of the innkeepers at The Park House (see page 151)

Pineapple Hill Bed & Breakfast

Kathy & Charles "Cookie" Triolo, Innkeepers
1324 River Road
New Hope, Pennsylvania 18938
(215) 862-1790
E-mail: ktriolo@pineapplehill.com

In the 1700s it was customary to place a pineapple on the front porch as a way of letting friends and neighbors know you were welcoming guests; this tradition continues at this Buck's County home. A full gourmet breakfast is skillfully prepared and served at individual candle-lit tables. This recipe is a real sweet treat for guests on sugar-restricted diets.

YUMMY BAKED GRAPEFRUIT
4 servings

2 large grapefruit, halved and sectioned   2 packets sugar substitute
1/2 teaspoon cinnamon

1. Preheat oven to 350°.

2. Place grapefruit halves on a baking pan.

3. Mix cinnamon and sugar substitute together in a small bowl and sprinkle over grapefruit.

4. Bake for 10 minutes, then place under the broiler for 2 more minutes.

Calories per serving: 60 – Fat: 0 – Sodium: 4 mg.
For exchange diets, count: 1 fruit. – Preparation time: 5 minutes.
Baking time: 15 minutes.

Used with permission of the innkeepers at Pineapple Hill Bed & Breakfast

SOUTHERN SCALLOPED PINEAPPLE
18 squares

nonstick cooking spray
1/4 cup soft margarine
1 1/2 cups sugar
3 eggs or 3/4 cup liquid egg substitute
20-ounce can pineapple chunks in juice, drained

80-ounce can crushed pineapple in juice, undrained
1/2 cup evaporated skim milk
5 cups white crustless bread cubes

1. Spray an 11 x 7-inch baking dish with cooking spray.

2. Cream margarine and sugar with mixer. Add eggs and beat well. Add pineapple, milk, and bread cubes, and stir well. Pour into prepared baking dish.

3. Cover with plastic wrap and refrigerate overnight.

4. In the morning, bake uncovered at 350° approximately 1 hour and 15 minutes or till set and lightly browned.

Calories per serving: 146 – Fat: 3 g. – Sodium: 122 mg.
For exchange diets, count: 1 starch, 1 fruit. – Preparation time: 20 minutes.
Refrigeration time: overnight. Baking time: 1 hour, 15 minutes.

Used with permission of the innkeepers at Hilton's Bluff Bed & Breakfast Inn

Hilton's Bluff Bed & Breakfast Inn

Jack & Norma Hilton, Innkeepers
2654 Valley Heights Drive
Pigeon Forge, Tennessee 37863
(423) 428-9765; Toll free: (800) 441-4188

This is a wonderful winter fruit dish to accompany ham or pork from Hilton's Bluff Bed & Breakfast Inn, a two-story country inn, high on a hilltop, nestled in a peaceful wooded setting. Awaken to the aroma of freshly-brewed coffee and partake of a leisurely southern gourmet breakfast served in the elegant, yet comfortable, dining room.

GEORGIA PEACH BREAKFAST TACO
8 servings

8 8-inch flour tortillas
2 tablespoons canola oil
CHEESE FILLING
   (best if prepared a day ahead):
1 cup cottage cheese
1/2 cup ricotta cheese
1 egg yolk
1/2 teaspoon vanilla
2 tablespoons sugar
1/2 teaspoon lemon zest
1/2 teaspoon orange zest

PEACH TOPPING:
8 fresh peaches, peeled and sliced thin
1/2 teaspoon vanilla
1/4 cup sugar
1 teaspoon creme de cassis (optional)

SUGGESTED PRESENTATION:
equal parts of nonfat sour cream
   and lemon yogurt
black currant syrup
toothpick

1. Combine all the ingredients for the cheese filling and refrigerate overnight.

2. Heat oil in a skillet over medium heat; brown tortillas lightly on both sides. While tortillas are still hot, fold into a hard-shell taco shape. Set tacos side by side in a baking dish to help retain shape and allow to cool.

3. Combine ingredients for the peach topping in a saucepan and cook on low heat for 15 minutes, stirring as peaches soften and mixture thickens.

4. For the final assembly, mix the sour cream with the yogurt. Select pretty dinner plates, and make a circle of the sour cream and yogurt around the outside edge of the plate. Next, make a circle of the black currant syrup toward the inside of the plate. Use a toothpick to trace through the mixture, creating a spider-web effect. Place the taco shell on the plate and fill with cheese and peaches, allowing them to spill onto the plate.

Calories per serving: 268 – Fat: 6 g. – Sodium: 603 mg.
For exchange diets, count: 2 starch, 1 fruit, 1 fat
Preparation time: 25 minutes. – Refrigeration time: overnight.

Used with permission of the innkeepers at The Old Garden Inn

The Old Garden Inn

Patty & Ron Gironda, Innkeepers
51 Temple Avenue
Newnan, Georgia 30263
(770) 304-0594;
Toll free: (800) 731-5011;
Fax: (770) 304-9003
www.communitynow.com/oldgarden

Patty Gironda says her guests come to The Old Garden Inn to refine the art of "fun living"—eating, drinking, relaxing, and enjoying comfortable beds and the gift of conversation. The elegant breakfast dishes are often low fat, but guests are never reminded! The inn itself features a romantic English cottage decor and the turn-of-the-century Greek Revival style would thrill Scarlett herself! The front porch renews the spirit and mornings begin with great coffee and orange juice with fruited ice cubes. For a final garnish to this recipe, Patty uses her deep purple violas from the porch.

Cereals

The Wildflower Inn

Ken & Sherrie Jern, Innkeepers
P.O. Box 11000
Jackson, Wyoming 83002
(307) 733-4710; Fax: (307) 739-0914
E-mail: 102744.2104@compuserve.com

The Wildflower Inn is a beautiful log home surrounded by aspens, ponds, and mountain views situated on three beautiful acres where you can truly experience Wyoming's gorgeous weather. In the spring, summer, and fall, guests have spectacular views of acres of wildflowers, birds, and the nearby mountains. Each morning brings freshly brewed coffee and tea, fresh juice, mountains of fruit, hot breads, and homemade jams, and perhaps a stack of blueberry-cornmeal pancakes or a hot, fragrant vegetable frittata. This refreshing muesli or homemade granola awaits the early riser.

APPLE MUESLI
4 1/2-cup servings

1 cup old-fashioned rolled oats	1/3 cup sliced almonds
3/4 cup apple juice	1/3 cup diced fresh apple
2 tablespoons vanilla yogurt	

1. Mix all ingredients together, and chill until very cold, 30 minutes or so.

Calories per serving: 130 – Fat: 4 g. – Sodium: 58 mg.
For exchange diets, count: 1 starch, 1 fat.
Preparation time: 10 minutes. – Chilling time: 30 minutes.

Used with permission of the innkeepers at The Wildflower Inn

The Kingsley House Bed & Breakfast

Gary & Kari King, Innkeepers
626 West Main Street
Fennville, Michigan 49408
(616) 561-6425; Fax: (616) 561-2593
E-mail: garyking@accn.org

This elegant Victorian mansion was built by Harvey Judson Kingsley for his wife, Eliza, and daughter, Carrie. Mr. Kingsley introduced apple trees to southwest Michigan. He did much work for Michigan State University. Breakfast features such goodies as honey-glazed pecan French toast, apple-sausage-cheddar quiche, and honey granola.

HONEY GRANOLA
12 1/2-cup servings

1/4 cup honey
1/4 cup soft margarine
pinch salt
1 1/2 teaspoons cinnamon
1/2 teaspoon vanilla

3 cups old-fashioned oats
1 cup flaked coconut
1/3 cup chopped walnuts
1/2 cup wheat germ
1/4 cup slivered almonds

1. Preheat oven to 275°.

2. Stir honey, margarine, salt, cinnamon, and vanilla until well blended.

3. Mix the oats, coconut, walnuts, wheat germ, and almonds in a greased 9 x 13-inch pan. Add butter mixture and stir to coat evenly.

4. Bake for 40 minutes, stirring often.

Calories per serving: 149 – Fat: 7 g. – Sodium: 70 mg.
For exchange diets, count: 1 starch, 1/2 fruit, 1 fat.
Preparation time: 15 minutes. – Baking time: 40 minutes.

Used with permission of the innkeepers at The Kingsley House Bed & Breakfast

LOW-FAT VANILLA GRANOLA
8 2/3-cup servings

2 cups old-fashioned oats
2 tablespoons light brown sugar
1 tablespoon ground cinnamon
1/3 cup apple juice concentrate

1 cup coconut
1 vanilla bean, split and seeded
1 cup dried sour cherries or cranberries
1 cup golden raisins

1. Preheat oven to 300°.

2. In large bowl, combine oats, sugar, cinnamon, and juice, and toss well. Spread on large cookie sheet and bake 25 minutes, stirring occasionally.

3. Stir in coconut and vanilla seeds and bake 25 minutes or till lightly browned.

4. Stir in cherries and raisins. Cool and store in airtight container for up to a month.

Calories per serving: 181 – Fat: 4 g. – Sodium: 273 mg.
For exchange diets, count: 2 starch, 1/2 fat.
Preparation time: 10 minutes. – Baking time: 50 minutes.

Used with permission of the innkeepers at Palisades Bed & Breakfast at Dash Point (see page 32)

OLD-WORLD GRANOLA
24 1/2-cup servings

6 cups rolled oats
1/2 cup wheat germ
1/4 cup sesame seeds
1/2 teaspoon salt
1/4 cup chopped pecans
1/4 cup untoasted sunflower seeds
1 teaspoon cinnamon

1 cup honey
1/4 cup vegetable oil
1/4 cup hot water
1 teaspoon vanilla
2 cups chopped dried fruit such as
    raisins, currants, cranberries,
    apricots, or pineapple

1. Preheat oven to 300°.

2. Combine oats, wheat germ, sesame seeds, salt, pecans, sunflower seeds, and cinnamon in a large mixing bowl.

3. Combine honey, oil, water, and vanilla, and pour over dry ingredients, stirring until evenly coated.

4. Spread mixture over two 15 x 8-inch baking sheets and bake for 25 minutes, stirring twice.

5. Cool and add dried fruit. Cover tightly.

Calories per serving: 186 – Fat: 5 g. – Sodium: 47 mg.
For exchange diets, count: 1 starch, 1 fruit, 1 fat.
Preparation time: 15 minutes. – Baking time: 25 minutes.

Used with permission of Juanita Loven, former innkeeper, Old World Inn

Old World Inn

Main Street
Spillville, Iowa 52168
Toll free: (800) 924-3739

Spillville is a Czechoslovakian community in northeast Iowa, and home of the Bily Brothers Clock Museum and Anton Dvorak Museum. The Old World Inn offers splendid hospitality as well as authentic Czech cuisine.

MIXED GRAIN AND WILD RICE CEREAL
16 1/2-cup servings

2 cups water
1/2 cup wild rice (or brown rice)
nonstick cooking spray
6 cups water
1/2 cup pearl barley
1/2 cup steel-cut oats (or regular
   oatmeal)

1/2 cup bulgur wheat
1/2 cup raisins
1/2 cup chopped pitted dates
1/4 cup firmly packed brown sugar
1 tablespoon butter
3/4 teaspoon salt
1/2 teaspoon ground cinnamon

1. Simmer rice in 2 cups of water about 20 minutes; drain.

2. Meanwhile, preheat oven to 375°.

3. Spray 2 1/2 quart ovenproof dish with cooking spray. Mix cooked rice with remaining 6 cups water. Stir in all remaining ingredients.

4. Cover loosely with foil and bake until grains are tender, water is absorbed, and cereal is creamy, stirring occasionally, about 1 1/2 hours.

Calories per serving: 91 – Fat: 1 g. – Sodium: 104 mg.
For exchange diets, count: 1 starch.
Preparation time: 20 minutes. – Baking time: 1 1/2 hours.

Used with permission of the innkeepers at Buttonwood Inn

Buttonwood Inn

Peter & Claudia Needham, Innkeepers
P.O. Box 1817
Mount Surprise Road
North Conway, New Hampshire 03860
(603) 356-2625;
Toll free: (800) 258-2625;
Fax: (603) 356-3140
E-mail: button_w@moose.ncia.net

As you drive up Mount Surprise Road, noise and stress are left behind. The Buttonwood Inn, originally constructed as a four-room cape-style farmhouse in 1820, is today a 10-room bed and breakfast offering private and shared baths and family suites. Each morning a full breakfast is provided featuring award-winning muffins and special entrées. Four course candlelight dinners are offered on a limited number of Saturdays during January and February.

GERMAN LEMON GRITS

8 servings

3/4 cup instant cream of wheat
4 cups skim milk
3 egg yolks or 1/2 cup liquid egg
   substitute

2 tablespoons lemon zest

1. Combine cream of wheat and milk in a microwave-safe bowl. Cook on high power for 8 minutes, stirring twice during cooking.

2. Stir in egg yolks or egg substitute and lemon zest. Microwave for 2 more minutes. Enjoy this dish hot now, or to serve later, pour grits into a square pan, cover and refrigerate.

3. When ready to serve, cut grits into 8 squares. Spray a no-stick skillet with butter-flavored spray. Warm squares in the skillet over low heat and serve.

Calories per serving: 119 – Fat: 0 – Sodium: 94 mg.
For exchange diets, count: 1 1/2 starch.
Preparation time: 20 minutes.

Used with permission of the innkeepers at The Hawkesdene House Bed & Breakfast Inn and Cottages

The Hawkesdene House Bed & Breakfast Inn and Cottages

Roy & Daphne Sargent, Innkeepers
Phillips Creek Road
Andrews, North Carolina 28901
(704) 321-6027;
Toll free: (800) 447-9549;
Fax: (704) 321-5007
E-mail: hawke@dnet.net

Special early breakfasts can be arranged for trout fishermen, hikers, or river runners that want to get an early start. The Hawkesdene House is a private home that combines all the charm and comfort of an English country house with the rustic beauty of the North Carolina mountains, nestled in a mountain cove adjoining the Nantahala National Forest.

Old Brewery Bed and Breakfast

Naser & Patricia Sharivar, Innkeepers
402 Bluff Street
Guttenberg, Iowa 52052
(319) 252-2094; Toll free: (800) 353-1307

This family of nationally-renowned artists shares
its time and talents with overnight guests. The
remodeled and restored 1858 stone brewery is a destination one never
forgets with a cave, beer and wine room, and forested walking trail. The
breakfast is all-Iowa—guests love this old family recipe.

BAKED OATMEAL

4 servings

nonstick cooking spray
1/2 teaspoon cinnamon
2 cups rolled oats
1/4 teaspoon salt
1 1/2 teaspoons baking powder
6 tablespoons applesauce

1/2 cup sugar
1/2 teaspoon vanilla
1/2 cup skim milk
1 egg or 1/4 cup liquid egg substitute
Garnish: raisins, pecans, and brown
sugar

1. Preheat oven to 350°.

2. Spray an 8-inch baking dish with cooking spray.

3. Mix cinnamon, oats, salt, and baking powder together in a mixing
bowl.

4. In another bowl, cream applesauce, sugar, vanilla, milk, and egg. Stir
in dry ingredients and transfer to the prepared pan. Sprinkle with
raisins, pecans, and brown sugar as desired.

5. Bake for 50 to 60 minutes. Serve as a cereal with milk or as a dessert
with fruit topping.

Calories per recipe: 276 – Fat: 3 g. – Sodium: 180 mg.
For exchange diets, count: 3 starch, 1/2 skim milk.
Preparation time: 15 minutes. – Baking time: 50 to 60 minutes.

Used with permission of the innkeepers at Old Brewery Bed and Breakfast

OATMEAL SOUFFLÉ
6 servings

nonstick cooking spray
1 cup skim milk
2 tablespoons butter-flavored
  margarine
3/4 cup quick-cooking oatmeal
1/3 cup reduced-fat cream cheese
1/4 teaspoon salt

1/2 cup brown sugar
1/2 teaspoon nutmeg
1/2 teaspoon cinnamon
3 eggs, separated
1/2 cup raisins
2 tablespoons chopped walnuts

1. Preheat oven to 325°.

2. Spray a 1 1/2 quart soufflé dish or casserole with cooking spray.

3. Measure milk and margarine into a small saucepan and heat until barely boiling. Slowly add the oatmeal, stirring constantly. Cook the oatmeal until thick, stirring often. Remove from heat and add cream cheese, salt, sugar, nutmeg, and cinnamon. Stir briskly to blend and smooth the mixture.

4. Beat the 3 egg yolks slightly and slowly add them to the oatmeal, stirring constantly. Stir in raisins and walnuts.

5. In a medium mixing bowl, beat the egg whites until stiff. Gently stir and fold the whites into the oatmeal mixture. Be careful not to over-fold. Spoon mixture into soufflé dish. Bake 35 to 40 minutes or until the soufflé is set. Serve warm.

Calories per serving: 229 – Fat: 8 g. – Sodium: 216 mg.
For exchange diets, count: 2 starch, 1 1/2 fat.
Preparation time: 20 minutes. – Baking time: 40 minutes.

Used with permission of the innkeepers at Tyrone Pike Bed & Breakfast

Tyrone Pike Bed & Breakfast

Tim, Jean, Carey, and Doug Foreman, Innkeepers
3820 Tyrone Pike
Versailles, Kentucky 40383
Toll free: (800) 736-7722
Fax: (606) 873-2408 (on request)
E-mail: tyronebb@uky.campus.mci.net

Tyrone Pike is a contemporary, eclectic style of bed and breakfast that includes a sleigh bed, a family suite with game room, and a luxurious suite with kitchenette. Guests are treated as royalty with hors d'oeuvres upon arrival. The scenic location is enhanced by a neighboring horse farm and the Bluegrass Scenic Railroad.

Swiss Oatmeal
6 servings

1 red apple, cored and coarsely chopped

1 yellow apple, cored and coarsely chopped

1/2 cup apple cider or unsweetened apple juice

1 cup quick-cooking rolled oats

1 tablespoon honey

1 cup plain low-fat yogurt

2 tablespoons sliced almonds

2 tablespoons raisins

1 tablespoon dark brown sugar

1. Put the chopped apples into a large bowl with the cider or apple juice and toss the apples to moisten them. Stir in the oats and honey, then add the yogurt, almonds, and raisins. Stir to combine the mixture well.

2. Serve the oatmeal in individual bowls; sprinkle each serving with 1/2 teaspoon of brown sugar.

3. This mixture may be kept in the refrigerator for up to 2 days.

Calories per serving : 160 – Fat: 3 – Sodium 29 mg.
For exchange diets, count: 2 starch.
Preparation time: 10 minutes.

Used with permission of the innkeepers at Night Swan Intracoastal B & B

Night Swan Intracoastal B & B

Martha & Chuck Nighswonger, Innkeepers
512 South Riverside Drive
New Smyrna Beach, Florida 32168
(904) 423-4940;
Toll free: (800) 465-4261;
Fax: (904) 427-2814
E-mail: nightswanb@aol.com

This spacious three-story home has kept its character and charm of 1906 in the Historic District of New Smyrna Beach. With central fireplace, antique baby grand piano, and intricate, natural wood in every room, the Night Swan overlooks the Atlantic Intracoastal Waterway. Full breakfast is served in the dining room, or guests can enjoy a continental breakfast delivered to their room, the porch, or the dock. Low-fat/low-cholesterol cuisine is a specialty.

PUFF CEREAL

4 1/2-cup servings

1 tablespoon margarine
1/4 cup sugar
1 teaspoon grated lemon rind
2 egg yolks
3 tablespoons lemon juice
2 tablespoons flour

1/4 cup Post Grape-Nuts cereal
1 cup skim milk
2 egg whites, beaten until stiff
Garnish: whipped cream and
    Grape-Nuts

1. Preheat oven to 325°.

2. Cream margarine with sugar and lemon rind in a mixing bowl. Add egg yolks; beat until light and fluffy. Blend in lemon juice, flour, cereal, and milk. (Mixture will look curdled.)

3. Fold in beaten egg whites. Pour into 5 greased custard cups; place cups in pan of hot water.

4. Bake for about 40 minutes or until tops spring back when touched. Garnish with whipped cream and sprinkle with Grape-Nuts.

Calories per serving: 192 – Fat: 5 g. – Sodium: 243 mg.
For exchange diets, count: 1 starch, 1 fruit, 1 fat.
Preparation time: 15 minutes. – Baking time: 40 minutes.

Used with permission of the innkeepers at Hillside Farm B & B

Hillside Farm B & B

Gary & Deb Lintner, Innkeepers
607 Eby Chiques Road
Mount Joy, Pennsylvania 17552
(717) 653-6697; Fax: (717) 653-5233
(call ahead first)
E-mail: hillside3@juno.com

Hillside Farm Bed & Breakfast is a farm home in a peaceful rural setting featuring an old farmhouse, barn, and other outbuildings. It was once a dairy farm and is still surrounded by one of the largest areas of farmland left of Lancaster County, which guarantees the guests a healthy measure of rest and relaxation. Built prior to 1863, the farmhouse is a two-and-a-half story brick building with a standard design of four main rooms on each floor. A full, country all-you-can-eat breakfast is served family-style every morning. Be sure to bring your appetite. Snacks are served all afternoon and evening.

* * *

Muffins, Breads,
Coffee Cakes,
and Scones

Eagles' Landing Bed and Breakfast

Roger & Connie Halvorson, Innkeepers
82 North Street
Marquette, Iowa 52159
(319) 873-2509

Guests enjoy a wonderful view of the Mississippi River from every room of this light and airy house. A sandy beach waits just outside the door and courtesy bicycles are available. Connie, an accomplished cook and my personal friend, offers a choice of typical American, German, and Norwegian breakfast fare.

APPLE STREUSEL MUFFINS
24 muffins

1 teaspoon baking powder
1 teaspoon soda
1/2 teaspoon salt
2 teaspoons cinnamon
2 1/2 cups flour
1/2 cup vegetable oil
1/2 cup nonfat sour cream
1/2 cup sugar
1/2 cup brown sugar
1 cup buttermilk
2 eggs or 1/2 cup liquid egg
　substitute
2 cups diced unpeeled apples

STREUSEL:
1/4 cup white sugar
1/4 cup brown sugar
1 teaspoon cinnamon
1/2 cup flour
1/4 cup reduced-fat margarine
1/2 teaspoon vanilla

24 pecans

1. Preheat oven to 350°. Line 24 muffin cups with cupcake papers or spray generously with nonstick cooking spray.

2. In a large mixing bowl, combine baking powder, soda, salt, cinnamon, and flour.

3. In another bowl, combine oil, sour cream, sugar, brown sugar, buttermilk, and eggs. Pour oil mixture into the dry ingredients and mix until no crumbs remain. Gently fold in apples.

4. Fill prepared muffin cups.

5. Combine ingredients for the streusel in a small bowl. Sprinkle on top of the muffins. Press a pecan into the center of each one. Bake for 15 to 20 minutes.

Calories per serving: 175 – Fat: 6 g. – Sodium: 205 mg.
For exchange diets, count: 1 starch, 1 fruit, 1 fat.
Preparation time: 20 minutes. – Baking time: 20 minutes.

Used with permission of the innkeepers at Eagles' Landing Bed and Breakfast

BERRY CREAM MUFFINS
24 muffins

4 cups all-purpose flour
1 1/2 cups sugar
2 teaspoons baking powder
1 teaspoon baking soda
1 teaspoon salt
3 cups fresh or frozen raspberries
  or blueberries

4 eggs, lightly beaten, or 1 cup liquid
  egg substitute
2 cups nonfat sour cream
1/2 cup vegetable oil
1/2 cup applesauce
1 teaspoon vanilla extract

1. Preheat oven to 400°. Line 24 muffin cups with cupcake papers.

2. In a large bowl, combine flour, sugar, baking powder, baking soda, and salt; add berries and toss gently.

3. In a large bowl, combine eggs or liquid egg substitute, sour cream, oil, applesauce, and vanilla; mix well. Stir into dry ingredients just until moistened.

4. Fill muffin cups two-thirds full. Bake for 20 to 25 minutes or until muffins test done.

Calories per serving: 155 – Fat: 4 g. – Sodium: 206 mg.
For exchange diets, count: 1 starch, 1 fat, 1/2 fruit.
Preparation time: 20 minutes. – Baking time: 25 minutes.

Used with permission of the innkeepers at Romancing the Past Bed & Breakfast

Romancing the Past Bed & Breakfast

Jim & Renee Yeager, Innkeepers
830 Court Street
Fulton, Missouri 65251
(573) 592-1996

This historical Queen Anne home, circa 1868, will charm you from the moment you step onto the parquet floor and through the burl walnut archway. The innkeepers' purpose: "to offer hospitality using the gifts we have received, to serve others faithfully, administering God's grace." (I Peter 4:9–10) Breakfast is bountiful and can be enjoyed by candlelight in the formal dining room.

CREAM CHEESE MUFFINS
12 small muffins

FILLING:
4 ounces reduced-fat cream cheese, softened
1/4 cup sugar
1/2 teaspoon grated lemon or orange peel
1/8 teaspoon vanilla

BATTER:
1 egg or 1/4 cup liquid egg substitute
3/4 cup skim milk
1/4 cup vegetable oil
1/4 cup nonfat sour cream
2 cups flour
1/3 cup sugar
1 tablespoon baking powder
1/2 teaspoon salt
GARNISH: powdered sugar

1. Preheat oven to 350°.

2. Mix filling ingredients together in a small bowl with an electric mixer. Set aside.

3. Spray muffin tins generously with cooking spray.

4. In a medium mixing bowl, beat egg, milk, oil, and sour cream; set aside.

5. In another bowl, mix together flour, sugar, baking powder, and salt until well blended.

6. Pour liquids, all at once, into flour mixture; stir until moistened.

7. Fill muffin cups about half full. Spoon 1 teaspoon filling onto batter. Top with batter to three-fourths full.

8. Bake 30 to 35 minutes. Don't brown; should be light in color. Roll hot muffins in powdered sugar.

Calories per serving: 178 – Fat: 6 g. – Sodium: 210 mg.
For exchange diets, count: 1 1/2 starch, 1 fat.
Preparation time: 20 minutes. – Baking time: 35 minutes.

Used with permission of the innkeepers at Thorpe House Country Inn (see page 67)

CRANBERRY ORANGE MUFFINS
30 muffins

3/4 cup dried cranberries or 8 ounces fresh cranberries
11-ounce can mandarin oranges, drained and juice reserved
5 cups flour
1 2/3 cups sugar
2 tablespoons baking powder

1 teaspoon salt
1/4 cup butter-flavored margarine
1/2 cup nonfat sour cream
1 2/3 cups orange juice
6 eggs or 1 1/2 cups liquid egg substitute
1 tablespoon grated orange peel

1. If using dried cranberries, soak for 15 minutes in juice from mandarin oranges. Preheat oven to 375°.

2. Prepare muffin tins by spraying generously with nonstick cooking spray or lining with cupcake papers.

3. In a large mixing bowl, combine flour, sugar, baking powder, and salt.

4. Melt margarine and whisk in sour cream, orange juice, eggs, and orange peel. Beat well.

5. Stir liquid into the dry ingredients and mix just until moist. Add drained cranberries and mandarin oranges.

6. Spoon into prepared muffin tins and bake for 25 to 30 minutes.

Calories per serving: 158 – Fat: 2 g. – Sodium: 120
For exchange diets, count: 2 starch.
Preparation time: 15 minutes. – Baking time: 30 minutes.

Used with permission of the innkeepers at Joshua Grindle Inn

Joshua Grindle Inn

Jim & Arlene Moorehead, Innkeepers
P.O. Box 647
Mendocino, California 95460
Toll free: (800) GRINDLE
E-mail: joshgrin@joshgrin.com
www.joshgrin.com

Come to this New England-style village for the rugged headlands and the redwoods rising from the sea. Start off with a sumptuous breakfast and fill your day with horseback riding, browsing the shops, walking along the beach, or reading by your fire.

FRENCH BREAKFAST MUFFINS
12 muffins

1/3 cup soft margarine
1/2 cup sugar
1 egg or 1/4 cup liquid egg substitute
1 1/2 cups flour
1 1/2 teaspoons baking powder
1/2 teaspoon salt

1/4 teaspoon nutmeg
1 1/2 cups skim milk
TOPPINGS:
2 tablespoons melted margarine
1/2 cup sugar + 1 teaspoon cinnamon

1. Preheat oven to 350°.

2. Line 12 muffin cups with papers or spray generously with nonstick cooking spray.

3. Mix margarine, sugar, and egg thoroughly. Stir in flour, baking powder, salt, and nutmeg.

4. Add milk and stir just until ingredients are blended. Fill prepared cups two-thirds full and bake for 20 minutes.

5. Remove muffins from oven and immediately roll in melted margarine and sugar and cinnamon mixture.

Calories per serving: 146 – Fat: 5 g. – Sodium: 116 mg.
For exchange diets, count: 1 starch, 1/2 fruit, 1 fat.
Preparation time: 15 minutes. – Baking time: 20 minutes.

Used with permission of Juanita Loven, former innkeeper, Old World Inn (see page 44)

MORNING GLORY MUFFINS
18 muffins

1 cup sugar
2 1/4 cups flour
1 tablespoon cinnamon
2 teaspoons baking soda
1/2 teaspoon salt
1/4 cup shredded coconut
1/2 cup golden raisins
1 apple with peeling, shredded

8 ounces crushed pineapple, drained well
2 cups grated carrots
3 eggs or 3/4 cup liquid egg substitute
1/3 cup vegetable oil
1/2 cup nonfat sour cream
1 teaspoon vanilla

1. Preheat oven to 350°. Prepare 18 muffin tins by lining with papers or spraying generously with nonstick cooking spray.

2. Mix sugar, flour, cinnamon, soda, and salt together in a large bowl. Fold in coconut, fruit, and carrots.

3. In a separate bowl, whisk eggs with oil, sour cream, and vanilla. Add egg mixture to dry ingredients and blend just until moist.

4. Fill prepared muffin cups three-fourths full. Bake for 35 minutes. Cool in pan for 10 minutes, then remove to a rack. These muffins freeze very well.

Calories per muffin: 168 – Fat: 4 g. – Sodium: 231 mg.
For exchange diets, count: 1 starch, 1 fruit, 1/2 fat.
Preparation time: 20 minutes. – Baking time: 35 minutes.

Used with permission of the innkeepers at Joy's Morning Glory Bed and Breakfast (see page 110)

OATMEAL MUFFINS
12 muffins

1 cup oatmeal
1 cup buttermilk
1/4 cup margarine
1/2 cup brown sugar
1 egg or 1/4 cup liquid egg
   substitute

1 cup flour
1 teaspoon baking powder
1/2 teaspoon soda
1/4 teaspoon salt

1. Preheat oven to 400°. Line muffin cups with papers or spray generously with nonstick cooking spray.

2. Soak oatmeal in the buttermilk for about an hour in a mixing bowl.

3. In a medium bowl, cream margarine and brown sugar. Add egg and beat well.

4. Add half of the flour and all of the baking powder, soda, and salt to the sugar and egg mixture. Beat well. Fold in the oatmeal. Add the remaining flour and mix just until all is moist.

5. Spoon into muffin cups and bake for 20 minutes.

Calories per serving: 126 – Fat: 3 g. – Sodium: 187 mg.
For exchange diets, count: 1 1/2 starch.
Soaking time: 1 hour – Preparation time: 15 minutes. – Baking time: 20 minutes.

Used with permission of the innkeepers at The Claytonian

The Claytonian

Don & Eileen Christensen, Innkeepers
100 South Front Street
Clayton, Iowa 52049
(319) 964-2776

Resting on the banks of the Mississippi River in Northeast Iowa, Claytonian guests can rock away the hours outside their suites and watch the river go by. The limestone bluffs along the riverbank of the northern Mississippi make for enchanted scenery. Watch a barge lock through Lock 10 just 10 minutes south. Or visit Pikes Peak State Park, a famous stop by Marquette and Joliet in their discovery of the west. The breakfast menus at this inn are all "good and plenty," including this favorite.

NO-SUGAR BANANA-ORANGE MUFFINS
18 muffins

2 cups flour
1 teaspoon baking soda
1 teaspoon baking powder
1 1/2 teaspoons pumpkin pie spice
1 cup mashed bananas
6 ounces orange juice

2 eggs or 1/2 cup liquid egg
  substitute
2 tablespoons unsweetened
  applesauce
1 cup raisins
1/4 cup chopped nuts

1. Preheat oven to 350°.

2. Line muffin tins with cupcake papers or spray with nonstick cooking spray.

3. In a large mixing bowl, blend first four ingredients.

4. In a small mixing bowl, mix together bananas, orange juice, eggs, and applesauce. Add this to the flour mixture and stir just until moist. Fold in raisins and nuts.

5. Fill prepared muffin tins three-fourths full and bake for 20 minutes.

Calories per serving: 116 – Fat: 2 g. – Sodium: 111 mg.
For exchange diets, count: 1 1/2 starch.
Preparation time: 20 minutes. – Baking time: 20 minutes.

Used with permission of the innkeepers at Bauer Haus Bed & Breakfast (see page 34)

RAISIN BRAN MUFFINS
36 muffins

4 beaten eggs or 1 cup liquid
  egg substitute
2 cups sugar
1 cup vegetable oil
1 quart buttermilk

5 teaspoons baking soda
2 teaspoons salt
5 cups flour
15-ounce package raisin bran cereal

1. Preheat oven to 400°.

2. Line muffin tins with cupcake papers or spray generously with non-stick cooking spray.

3. In a large bowl, mix together eggs, sugar, oil, and buttermilk. In another bowl, combine baking soda, salt, and flour. Add flour mixture to egg mixture, one cup at a time. Fold in raisin bran.

4. Spoon into muffin cups and bake for 20 minutes. Muffin batter keeps in refrigerator up to six weeks.

Calories per serving: 102 – Fat: 3 g. – Sodium: 282 mg.
For exchange diets, count: 1 starch, 1/2 fat.
Preparation time: 20 minutes. – Baking time: 20 minutes.

Used with permission of the innkeepers at The Hawkesdene House Bed & Breakfast
Inn and Cottages (see page 46)

STRAWBERRY-ORANGE MUFFINS
12 muffins

2 1/2 cups all-purpose flour
2 teaspoons baking powder
1 teaspoon baking soda
1/2 teaspoon salt
1/2 cup sugar
1/2 cup skim milk

1/2 cup nonfat sour cream
1/4 cup vegetable oil
1 egg or 1/4 cup liquid egg substitute
1 tablespoon finely grated orange zest
1 cup thinly sliced strawberries
1/3 cup all-fruit strawberry spread

1. Preheat oven to 400°.

2. Spray muffin tins with nonstick cooking spray or line with cupcake papers.

3. In a large bowl, stir together flour, baking powder, baking soda, and salt.

4. In a medium bowl, whisk together sugar, milk, sour cream, oil, egg, and orange zest until mixed. Stir in strawberries. Add to the dry ingredients and stir just until blended.

5. Place a spoonful of batter in each prepared muffin cup. Top each with a scant teaspoon of strawberry spread. Spoon the remaining batter over the spread, filling each cup about two-thirds full.

6. Bake until a toothpick inserted in the center of a muffin comes out clean, 15 to 18 minutes. Cool in tins for 5 minutes.

Calories per muffin: 206 – Fat: 5 g. – Sodium: 252 mg.
For exchange diets, count: 1 1/2 starch, 1 fat, 1/2 fruit.
Preparation time: 20 minutes. – Baking time: 18 minutes. – Cooling time: 5 minutes.

Used with permission of the innkeepers at Forget-Me-Not Bed & Breakfast

Forget-Me-Not Bed & Breakfast

Christa & Richard Grunert, Innkeepers
1467 North Elizabeth Scales Mound Road
Galena/Elizabeth, Illinois 61028
(815) 858-3744
E-mail: forget-me-not@juno.com

Welcome to a newly-built country home with old-world ambience. The Forget-Me-Not is located on 23 acres overlooking a forested valley and panoramic countryside away from the city stresses. It's only minutes away from historic Galena, Apple Canyon Lake, and Eagle Ridge Territory. There are many scenic routes in and around the area.

SWEET POTATO MUFFINS
18 muffins

DRY INGREDIENTS:
1 1/4 cups uncooked oats
1 cup flour
2 tablespoons chopped walnuts
1 teaspoon baking powder
1/2 teaspoon baking soda
1/2 teaspoon nutmeg
1/2 teaspoon cloves
1 teaspoon cinnamon
1/2 teaspoon salt
LIQUID INGREDIENTS:
1 cup mashed sweet potato or
   canned pumpkin

3/4 cup brown sugar
1/4 cup vegetable oil
1/4 cup nonfat sour cream
1/4 cup skim milk
1 egg or 1/4 cup liquid egg substitute
1 teaspoon vanilla
TOPPING:
1/4 cup oats
1/4 cup flour
1/4 cup brown sugar
1 tablespoon chopped pecans or walnuts
1 teaspoon cinnamon
2 tablespoons margarine

1. Preheat oven to 400°. Line muffin tins with cupcake papers or spray with nonstick cooking spray.

2. Combine dry ingredients in a large mixing bowl.

3. In a medium mixing bowl, combine liquid ingredients.

4. Add liquid ingredients to dry ingredients, stirring just until moistened; do not overmix.

5. Mix topping ingredients in a small mixing bowl.

6. Fill muffin tins two-thirds full. Sprinkle with topping.

7. Bake for 15 to 20 minutes.

Calories per serving: 155 – Fat: 5 g. – Sodium: 106 mg.
For exchange diets, count: 2 starch.
Preparation time: 15 minutes. – Baking time: 20 minutes.

Used with permission of the innkeepers at The Brewster Inn (see page 167)

BISHOP'S BREAD
1 loaf or 18 slices

3 cups reduced-fat biscuit mix
1/2 cup sugar
1 egg or 1/4 cup liquid egg substitute
1 tablespoon grated orange peel
1 1/4 cups fresh orange juice
3 tablespoons vegetable oil

1/4 cup wheat germ
1/2 cup reduced-fat semi-sweet
   chocolate chips
1/4 cup raisins
1/4 cup chopped nuts

1. Preheat oven to 350°.

2. Combine biscuit mix and sugar in large mixing bowl.

3. In a separate bowl, combine egg, orange peel, orange juice, and oil.

4. Add egg mixture to biscuit mix and beat with a wooden spoon until mixture is smooth. Stir in wheat germ. Fold in 1/4 cup chocolate chips, raisins, and nuts.

5. Turn into greased 9 x 5 x 3-inch loaf pan. Sprinkle remaining 1/4 cup chocolate chips on top of batter. Bake 55 to 60 minutes or until wooden pick inserted into center comes out clean. Turn out of pan and cool completely on wire rack.

Calories per slice: 216 – Fat: 6 g. – Sodium: 373
For exchange diets, count: 2 starch, 1 fat.
Preparation time: 20 minutes. – Baking time: 60 minutes.

Used with permission of the innkeepers at Doll House Inn Historical Bed & Breakfast

Doll House Inn Historical Bed & Breakfast

Barbara & Joe Gerovac, Innkeepers
709 East Ludington Avenue
Ludington, Michigan 49431
(616) 843-2286; Toll free: (800) 275-4616

The parlor and living room of this Victorian inn are filled with interesting finds from the innkeepers' travels and include an antique doll collection with many reproductions made by Barb. The home has fine hardwood floors, beautiful woodwork and even pillars in the parlor, and airy 10-foot ceilings throughout. Light and air are dominant themes in this old home and fine lacy curtains cover windows to let in the natural light.

The best part of the morning is a hearty breakfast with plenty of hot coffee and good conversation. Guests may stay for two weeks and not repeat a meal. Barb likes making Bishop's Bread because she doesn't have to get out the mixer!

CINNAMON CUSTARD SWIRL BREAD
2 loaves, 16 slices each

5 to 5 1/2 cups all-purpose flour,
   divided
2 packages active dry yeast
   (2 tablespoons)
3-ounce package egg custard mix
1 teaspoon salt
1 cup milk

1/2 cup water
1/4 cup margarine, divided
2 eggs or 1/2 cup liquid egg substitute
1/2 cup sugar
1 tablespoon plus 1 teaspoon
   cinnamon
butter-flavored spray

1. Combine 2 cups flour, yeast, custard mix, and salt in a large mixing bowl. Mix well.

2. Heat milk, water, and 2 tablespoons margarine in saucepan until warm.

3. Add milk mixture and eggs or egg substitute to flour mixture. Blend at low speed until moistened, then for 3 minutes at medium speed.

4. Stir in enough remaining flour to make a firm dough. Knead on floured board until smooth and elastic (5 to 8 minutes). Place in greased bowl, turning to grease top. Cover and let rise in warm place until doubled in bulk (about 1 hour).

5. To prepare filling, combine sugar with 1 tablespoon cinnamon, and set aside.

6. Punch dough down and divide into two parts. On lightly floured surface, roll each half to a 14- by 7-inch rectangle.

7. Spread each with 1 tablespoon softened butter and sprinkle with sugar and cinnamon filling. Roll up tightly, pressing dough into roll with each turn. Pinch ends and edges to seal.

8. Place in greased 9 x 5-inch loaf pans. Sprinkle with remaining teaspoon of cinnamon. Cover and let rise in warm place until doubled in bulk (about 1 hour). Bake at 375° for 35 to 40 minutes.

9. Spray tops of loaves with butter-flavored spray. Remove from pans and cool on a rack.

Suggestion: Use leftover bread for French toast.

Calories per serving: 104 – Fat: 2 g. – Sodium: 78 mg.
For exchange diets, count: 1 1/2 starch.
Preparation time: 25 minutes. – Rising time: 2 risings for a total of 2 hours.
Baking time: 40 minutes.

Used with permission of the innkeepers at 1874 Stonehouse Bed & Breakfast on Mulberry Hill

1874 Stonehouse Bed & Breakfast on Mulberry Hill

Dan & Carrie Riggs, Innkeepers
RR 1, Box 67A
Cottonwood Falls, Kansas 66845
(316) 273-8481; Fax: (316) 273-8481
E-mail: SHMH1874@aol.com

This 1874 Stonehouse is a haven for birders, naturalists, hikers, cyclists, equestrians, hunters, fishermen, antique collectors, and historians. Breakfasts will leave guests with memories of a simpler, less hurried time in a place where Kansas history and one of its pioneer families left their legacy.

Old Thyme Inn Bed & Breakfast

George & Marcia Dempsey, Innkeepers
779 Main Street
Half Moon Bay, California 94019-1924
(415) 726-1616; Fax: (415) 726-6394
E-mail: oldthyme@coastside.net

This Queen Anne Victorian bed and breakfast has seven private rooms, most with fireplaces and/or double-whirlpool tubs. All the rooms have antiques, fresh-cut flowers, and resident teddy bears. A fragrant English herb garden with over 50 varieties of herbs and flowers provides a tranquil setting for the inn. The Old Thyme Inn is located a short walk from the beach 40 minutes south of San Francisco on Highway 1.

GEORGE'S FAMOUS BANANA BREAD

16 slices

2 cups all-purpose flour
1 cup sugar
1 teaspoon baking soda
1 teaspoon baking powder
1/2 teaspoon salt
2 eggs or 1/2 cup liquid egg
   substitute

3 large ripe bananas, mashed
1/4 cup canola oil
1/2 cup plus 1 tablespoon buttermilk
1 teaspoon vanilla extract
2 tablespoons chopped walnuts

1. Preheat oven to 350°.

2. In a large bowl, stir together flour, sugar, baking soda, baking powder, and salt.

3. In another mixing bowl, combine eggs or egg substitute, bananas, oil, buttermilk, and vanilla. Add egg mixture to flour mixture, stirring just until combined.

4. Pour into a greased 9 x 5 x 3-inch loaf pan. Sprinkle walnuts on top. Bake for approximately 1 hour or until it tests done.

Calories per serving: 112 – Fat: 4 g. – Sodium: 186 mg.
For exchange diets, count: 1 starch, 1 fat.
Preparation time: 15 minutes. – Baking time: 1 hour.

Used with permission of the innkeepers at Old Thyme Inn & Breakfast

JALAPEÑO AND SAGE WHOLE WHEAT CORN BREAD
16 slices

nonstick cooking spray
1/4 cup reduced-fat margarine
1/4 cup brown sugar
1 egg or 1/4 cup liquid egg substitute
1 cup skim milk
2/3 cup whole wheat flour
2/3 cup flour

2/3 cup cornmeal
2 teaspoons baking powder
1/2 teaspoon sage
1/2 teaspoon salt
1/4 cup finely chopped jalapeño
   peppers

1. Preheat oven to 375°.

2. Spray a loaf pan with cooking spray.

3. In a medium bowl, cream margarine and brown sugar. Add egg and milk, and stir.

4. In another bowl, combine flours, cornmeal, baking powder, sage, and salt. Add to egg mixture and stir just to combine. Fold in peppers.

5. Bake for 35 minutes.

Calories per serving: 108 – Fat: 3 g. – Sodium: 224 mg.
For exchange diets, count: 1 1/2 starch.
Preparation time: 20 minutes. – Baking time: 35 minutes.

Used with permission of the innkeepers at Parson's Inn Bed and Breakfast (see page 28)

LEMON YOGURT BREAD
2 loaves, 16 slices per loaf

3 cups flour
1 teaspoon baking soda
1/2 teaspoon baking powder
1 teaspoon salt
3 eggs or 3/4 cup liquid egg substitute

1/2 cup vegetable oil
1/4 cup nonfat sour cream
1 1/2 cups sugar
2 cups lemon yogurt
2 tablespoons fresh-squeezed lemon
   juice

1. Preheat oven to 325°.

2. Sift the dry ingredients in a medium bowl. Lightly beat the eggs in a large bowl. Add oil, sour cream, and sugar; mix well. Add yogurt and lemon juice, and mix thoroughly.

3. Add dry ingredients to yogurt mixture; mix well. Pour into two well-greased loaf pans. Bake for 1 hour.

Calories per serving: 105 – Fat: 2 g. – Sodium: 131 mg.
For exchange diets, count: 1 1/2 starch.
Preparation time: 20 minutes. – Baking time: 1 hour.

Used with permission of the innkeepers at Sherwood Forest B & B (see page 81)

The Log House & Homestead on Spirit Lake

**Yvonne & Lyle Tweten
and daughter Suzanne, Innkeepers
P.O. Box 130
Vergas, Minnesota 56587
(218) 342-2318; Toll free: (800) 342-2318**

This hostelry is located in picturesque Otter Tail County in the heart of Minnesota's west central lakes region. Breakfast is meant to be an experience. This bountiful meal occurs in front of the fire or on the screen porch at the Log House. At the Homestead, service is in-room on linen-dressed tea carts, while the Suite has a private breakfast room. Fresh-squeezed orange juice and fresh-ground coffee are "de rigueur."

PUMPKIN BREAD
2 loaves, 16 slices each

nonstick cooking spray
3 1/2 cups flour
2 cups sugar
2 teaspoons soda
1 1/2 teaspoons salt
1 teaspoon cinnamon
1 teaspoon ginger
1 teaspoon cloves

1 teaspoon nutmeg
1/4 cup vegetable oil
1/2 cup nonfat sour cream
4 eggs or 1 cup liquid egg substitute
2/3 cup water
15-ounce can Libby's pumpkin (other brands are too watery)
TOPPING: 2 tablespoons chopped nuts

1. Preheat oven to 350°.

2. Spray two loaf pans with cooking spray.

3. Sift dry ingredients together in a large mixing bowl.

4. Beat together remaining ingredients and then combine with dry ingredients. Mix until smooth.

5. Pour into prepared pans, sprinkle with nuts, and bake for 55 to 60 minutes or until a wooden tester comes out clean.

Calories per serving: 132 – Fat: 3 g. – Sodium: 196 mg.
For exchange diets, count: 1 starch, 1 fruit.
Preparation time: 15 minutes. – Baking time: 60 minutes

Used with permission of the innkeepers at The Log House & Homestead on Spirit Lake

SPICED RHUBARB BREAD
2 loaves, 16 slices each

1 1/3 cups packed brown sugar
1/2 cup vegetable oil
1 large egg or 1/4 cup liquid egg
   substitute
1 cup buttermilk
1 teaspoon vanilla extract
1 teaspoon baking soda
1 teaspoon baking powder
2 1/2 cups all-purpose flour

1 teaspoon salt
1 teaspoon cinnamon
1 1/2 cups diced fresh or frozen
   rhubarb
TOPPING:
2 tablespoons chopped nuts
1/3 cup sugar
1 tablespoon melted margarine
1 teaspoon ground cinnamon

1. Preheat oven to 350°.

2. In a mixing bowl, beat brown sugar, oil, and egg. Add buttermilk, vanilla, baking soda, and baking powder; mix well.

3. Combine flour, salt, and cinnamon; stir into mixture. Fold in rhubarb.

4. Pour into two greased 8 1/2 x 4 1/2-inch loaf pans.

5. Combine topping ingredients and sprinkle over batter; bake for 1 hour or until bread tests done.

Calories per slice: 118 – Fat: 5 g. – Sodium: 129 mg.
For exchange diets, count: 1 starch, 1 fat.
Preparation time: 20 minutes. – Baking time: 1 hour.

Used with permission of the innkeepers at The Seymour Bed & Breakfast

The Seymour Bed & Breakfast

Tom & Gwen Paton, Innkeepers
1248 Blue Star Highway
South Haven, Michigan 49090
(616) 227-3918; Fax: (616) 227-3010
E-mail: seymour@cybersol.com

Experience tranquillity on 11 acres of beautiful Michigan countryside 1/2 mile from Lake Michigan. Tom is a former restaurateur and Gwen is a hobbyist potter and photographer. Her works, and other gift items, are offered for sale at the inn.

STICKY CARAMEL ROLLS
12 wedges

nonstick cooking spray
1/4 cup sliced almonds
1/4 cup soft margarine
2 tablespoons corn syrup

1 cup brown sugar
2 tablespoons water
2 cans reduced-fat crescent rolls

1. Preheat oven to 350°.

2. Spray Bundt pan generously with cooking spray.

3. Sprinkle almonds over the bottom of the pan.

4. Heat margarine, corn syrup, brown sugar, and water in a saucepan until it boils, stirring occasionally.

5. Remove rolls from cans in sections. They will be rolled up. Do not unroll. Cut each section into 4 mini-rolls. Arrange 8 slices in the pan, separating slightly. Spoon half of the syrup over rolls. Repeat with remaining rolls and sauce.

6. Bake for 30 minutes until golden brown. Let stand for 3 minutes, then turn out onto a serving plate. Slice into wedges to serve.

Calories per serving: 181 – Fat: 5 g. – Sodium: 372 mg.
For exchange diets, count: 1 starch, 1 fruit, 1 fat.
Preparation time: 20 minutes. – Baking time: 30 minutes.
Cooling time: 3 minutes in pan.

Used with permission of the innkeepers at The Claytonian (see page 57)

Thorpe House Country Inn

Mike & Jean Owens, Innkeepers
P.O. Box 36
19049 Clayborne Street
Metamora, Indiana 47030-0036
(317) 647-5425

Circa 1840–1860, this peaceful, easy feeling inn is a typical middle-class clapboard with a "gingerbready" front porch. It's located only one block from the restored Whitewater Canal. Casual, cozy guest rooms are furnished with antiques and country touches. There is no in-room telephone, television, radio, or alarm clock to interrupt your relaxation. Enjoy a hearty breakfast before exploring over 100 shops, galleries, and museums in this quaint historic village, listed on the National Register.

SWEET ROLLS
36 rolls

2 packages dry yeast
1 tablespoon sugar
1 cup lukewarm water
1 cup skim milk
6 tablespoons soft margarine
1/2 cup sugar
1/2 teaspoon salt
3 eggs, beaten, or 3/4 cup liquid
  egg substitute

6 1/2 cups flour
1/4 cup flour for kneading
nonstick cooking spray
3 tablespoons soft margarine
2 teaspoons cinnamon
1/2 cup brown sugar

1. Dissolve yeast and 1 tablespoon sugar in lukewarm water. Let stand for at least 15 minutes.

2. Meanwhile, in a mixing bowl, heat milk and 6 tablespoons margarine in microwave for 1 minute. Add sugar, salt, and beaten eggs. Stir in yeast mixture. Add flour, 2 cups at a time, mixing between additions.

3. Knead until soft and smooth (about 7 minutes), then shape into a ball. Spray the dough with cooking spray and place in a mixing bowl. Cover with a clean towel and allow to rise in a warm area for 1 1/2 hours.

4. Punch down, knead 10 to 15 times on a floured surface, and then allow to rise again for 1 hour.

5. Punch down second time and place on floured board. Roll into 12- by 14-inch rectangle. Spread with margarine and sprinkle with cinnamon and brown sugar. Roll dough up tightly and cut into 3/4-inch wheels. Place on baking sheet that has been sprayed with cooking spray. Allow rolls to rise 45 minutes in a warm place.

6. Preheat oven to 350°. Bake for 15 minutes or until lightly browned. Cool 10 minutes, then remove to a rack.

Calories per serving: 155 – Fat: 3 g. – Sodium: 109 mg.
For exchange diets, count: 1 1/2 starch, 1/2 fat.
Preparation time: 30 minutes. – Rising time: 3 hours. – Baking time: 15 minutes.

Used with permission of the innkeepers at Parson's Inn Bed and Breakfast (see page 28)

ZESTY CINNAMON ROLL-UPS

16 servings, 2 rolls each

8-ounce package reduced-fat
   cream cheese, softened
1 egg yolk
1/4 cup sugar
1 to 2 teaspoons grated orange zest

1 loaf thin-sliced sandwich bread
1/2 cup brown sugar, firmly packed
1 to 2 teaspoons cinnamon
2 tablespoons margarine, melted

1. Preheat the oven to 350°.

2. Mix the softened cream cheese, egg yolk, sugar, and orange zest.

3. Remove the crusts from the bread slices. (Save the crusts for another use or feed the birds!) Flatten a slice with rolling pin and spread with a spoonful of the cream cheese mixture. Roll up and seal edges by pinching together. Set aside with the sealed side down and continue until all slices are done.

4. Mix together the brown sugar and cinnamon in a shallow bowl and place the melted margarine in another shallow bowl. Cut each bread roll in half, making 2 smaller rolls.

5. Roll each half quickly in the melted margarine and then in the sugar mixture. Place on a greased cookie sheet. (This is a messy process but it can be done ahead of time. They can be frozen at this point too.)

6. Bake the rolls for 15 to 20 minutes. Remove and serve warm with slices of a firm, slightly tart apple.

Calories per serving: 155 – Fat: 5 g. – Sodium: 234 mg.
For exchange diets, count: 2 starch.
Preparation time: 30 minutes. – Baking time: 20 minutes.

Used with permission of the innkeepers at Plantation House

Plantation House

Merland & Barbara Clark, Innkeepers
401 Plantation Street
RR 2, Box 17
Elgin, Nebraska 68636-9301
(402) 843-2287
E-mail: plantation@gpcom.net
www.bbonline.com/ne/nabb

This three-diamond-rated Greek-Revival mansion sits at the edge of the small town of Elgin and offers you historic elegance and comfort. A full breakfast might feature French toast and home-cured bacon or egg/cheese puff with sausage.

CARAMEL ROLLS
36 rolls

2 packages dry yeast
1 tablespoon sugar
1 cup lukewarm water
1 cup skim milk
6 tablespoons soft margarine
1/2 cup sugar
1/2 teaspoon salt
3 eggs, beaten, or 3/4 cup liquid
   egg substitute
6 1/2 cups flour

1/4 cup flour for kneading
nonstick cooking spray
3 tablespoons soft margarine
2 teaspoons cinnamon
1/2 cup brown sugar

CARAMEL TOPPING:
6 tablespoons soft margarine
1/3 cup brown sugar
3/4 cup chopped pecans

1. Dissolve yeast and 1 tablespoon sugar in lukewarm water. Let stand for at least 15 minutes.

2. Meanwhile, in a mixing bowl, heat milk and 6 tablespoons margarine in microwave for 1 minute. Add sugar, salt, and beaten eggs. Stir in yeast mixture. Add flour, 2 cups at a time, mixing between additions.

3. Knead until soft and smooth (about 7 minutes), then shape into a ball. Spray the dough with cooking spray and place in the mixing bowl. Cover with a clean towel and allow to rise in a warm area for 1 1/2 hours.

4. Punch down, knead 10 to 15 times on a floured surface and then allow to rise again for 1 hour.

5. Meanwhile, combine ingredients for caramel topping in a mixing bowl and microwave for 30 seconds. Stir until smooth and pour into the bottom of a 9- x 13-inch pan.

6. Punch down dough a second time and place on floured board. Roll into 12- by 14-inch rectangle. Spread with margarine, and sprinkle with cinnamon and brown sugar. Roll dough up tightly and cut into 3/4-inch wheels. Place over caramel topping and allow rolls to rise 45 minutes in a warm place.

7. Preheat oven to 350°. Bake for 15 minutes or until lightly browned. Cool 10 minutes, then invert onto a serving platter or storage container.

Calories per serving: 202 – Fat: 7 g. – Sodium: 121 mg.
For exchange diets, count: 2 starch, 1 fat.
Preparation time: 30 minutes. – Rising time: 3 hours. – Baking time: 15 minutes.

Used with permission of the innkeepers at Parson's Inn Bed and Breakfast (see page 28)

BUTTERMILK SAGE BREADSTICKS
14 breadsticks

2 cups flour
1 tablespoon sugar
2 tablespoons rubbed sage
1 teaspoon baking powder
1/2 teaspoon salt
1/2 teaspoon ground red pepper

1 package 50%-faster-rising dry
   yeast
1 tablespoon margarine
1 cup very warm nonfat buttermilk
2 teaspoons nonfat buttermilk
nonstick cooking spray

1. Place first seven ingredients in a large mixing bowl and blend with a whisk.

2. Cut in margarine and slowly add warm buttermilk. Stir until the dough leaves the sides of the bowl and forms a ball.

3. Turn dough out onto a floured board and knead lightly six times, shaping into a ball.

4. Roll dough into a 14- by 6-inch rectangle and cut dough into 14 1-inch strips. Brush the strips with buttermilk.

5. Gently pick up both ends of the strip and twist. Place on nonstick baking sheet sprayed with cooking spray. Cover and let rise in a warm place about 20 minutes or until puffy.

6. Bake at 425° for 8 minutes or until golden.

Calories per serving: 82 – Fat: 1 g. – Sodium: 105 mg.
For exchange diets, count: 1 starch.
Preparation time: 20 minutes. – Rising time: 20 minutes. – Baking time: 8 minutes.

Used with permission of the innkeepers at Peacock Hill Country Inn

Peacock Hill Country Inn

Walter & Anita Ogilvie, Innkeepers
6994 Giles Hill Road
College Grove, Tennessee 37046
(615) 368-7727 for information;
(800) 327-6663 for reservations

Perched atop a gentle hill on a two-lane road that winds through rolling farmland, Peacock Hill Country Inn welcomes its guests to Tennessee with luxurious accommodations, delightful meals, and accessibility to the shopping, fine dining, and entertainment attractions of Nashville and historic Williamson County.

FRENCH BREAD
2 loaves, 16 slices each

5 teaspoons yeast
2 teaspoons salt
2 cups water

6 cups bread flour
nonstick cooking spray

1. Combine yeast, salt, and water in mixing bowl.

2. Add flour and mix with electric dough hook for 5 minutes.

3. Spray another large mixing bowl with cooking spray. Remove dough and place in bowl. Cover with plastic wrap and allow to rise until doubled in size, about an hour.

4. Form dough into two long, cylindrical loaves. Place in French bread pans. Gash with sharp knife diagonally, 3 to 5 times. Cover with towel and allow to rise until doubled again, about 45 minutes.

5. Bake at 425° for 20 minutes.

Calories per slice: 85 – Fat: 0 – Sodium: 133 mg.
For exchange diets, count: 1 starch.
Preparation time: 15 minutes. – Rising time: 1 hour, 45 minutes.
Baking time: 20 minutes.

Used with permission of the innkeepers at The Inn at Battle Creek Bed and Breakfast

The Inn at Battle Creek Bed and Breakfast

Rod & Nancy Pearson, Innkeepers
P. O. Box 58
201 Maple Street
Battle Creek, Iowa 51006
(712) 365-4949

This elegantly restored 1899 Queen Anne Victorian Country Inn on the National Register of Historic Places showcases period antiques and original brass light fixtures in each room. A large terry-cloth bathrobe is provided for each guest.

ITALIAN CRACKED WHEAT BREAD
1 loaf, 16 slices

1/4 cup cracked wheat or bulgur
3/4 cup boiling water
1 cup warm water (105-115°)
1 teaspoon yeast
2 teaspoons honey
1 cup cool water
1 cup whole wheat flour

1 1/2 cups bread flour
1 teaspoon salt
2 cups all-purpose flour

TOPPING:
1 egg & 1 teaspoon water,
  beaten together

1. Pour boiling water over cracked wheat or bulgur in a small bowl; set aside for later use.

2. In a large mixing bowl, combine warm water, yeast, and honey. Let sit until bubbly (approximately 10 minutes).

3. Add cool water, whole wheat flour, and bread flour. Mix until smooth.

4. Loosely cover with plastic wrap and let sit in a warm place for 3 hours. Increase rising time to 4 hours if dough is not in a warm place. The dough may have to be punched down.

5. Add cracked wheat, salt, and enough all-purpose flour to make a sticky dough that barely holds its shape. Turn onto floured surface and knead, adding enough flour to keep from sticking, until elastic. Cover and let rest for 1/2 hour.

6. Form dough into desired loaf shapes and place on greased baking sheets. Let rise in a warm place until double in size (about 1/2 hours).

Buckhorn Inn

Rachael Young, Innkeeper
2140 Tudor Mountain Road
Gatlinburg, Tennessee 37738
(423) 436-4668

A gem from the past in the heart of the Smokies, Buckhorn Inn has managed to preserve what people originally came to this part of the country to enjoy. There is an abundance of natural beauty in a peaceful setting. The recipe was originated by Chef Bob Neisler.

7. Preheat oven to 450°. Cut diagonal slices on top of loaves. Brush with egg-water mixture. Bake 10 minutes, then turn oven down to 400°. Bake approximately 20 more minutes or until golden brown and hollow sounding when tapped. Cool on rack.

Calories per slice: 100 – Fat: 0 – Sodium: 133 mg.
For exchange diets, count: 1 1/2 starch.
Preparation time: 15 minutes. – Total rising time: 5 hours. – Baking time: 30 minutes.

Used with permission of the innkeeper at Buckhorn Inn (see previous page)

BLACK FOREST COFFEE CAKE
24 squares

nonstick cooking spray
3 eggs or 3/4 cup liquid egg substitute
1 cup sugar
1/4 cup vegetable oil
1/4 cup nonfat sour cream
1 1/2 cups skim milk
2 tablespoons vanilla
3 cups flour
2 teaspoons baking powder
1/2 cup reduced-fat chocolate chips

1 can light cherry pie filling

TOPPING:
1/2 cup reduced-fat baking mix
1/4 cup sugar
2 tablespoons reduced-fat margarine

GARNISH: 1/4 cup reduced-fat
chocolate chips

1. Preheat oven to 375°.

2. Spray a 9 x 13-inch baking pan with cooking spray.

3. In a large mixing bowl, beat eggs well; add sugar, oil, sour cream, milk, and vanilla. Beat in flour and baking powder.

4. Fold in chocolate chips. Pour into prepared pan.

5. Drop cherry pie filling by the teaspoon over the batter.

6. Blend ingredients for topping with a pastry blender to form loose crumbs. Sprinkle over top of cake and garnish with chocolate chips.

7. Bake for 50 to 60 minutes until golden brown.

Calories per serving: 181 – Fat: 5 g. – Sodium: 102 mg.
For exchange diets, count: 1 starch, 1 fat.
Preparation time: 20 minutes. – Baking time: 1 hour.

*Used with permission of the innkeeper at Bechtel Victorian Mansion Bed & Breakfast Inn
(see page 79)*

Bay Avenue's Sunset Bed & Breakfast

Al Longo & Joyce Tribble, Innkeepers
108 Bay Avenue
Cape Charles, Virginia 23310
(757) 331-2424;
Toll free: (888) 4BAYAVE;
Fax: (757) 331-4877
E-mail: SunsetBnB@aol.com

This 1915 Victorian B & B is located directly on beautiful Chesapeake Bay. Relax and unwind in what we lovingly call the "Cape Charles time warp," where there are no traffic lights, no parking meters, and no parking problems. Or take one of the inn's bicycles for a spin around town.

BLUEBERRY STREUSEL COFFEE CAKE

12 squares

nonstick cooking spray
2 cups all-purpose flour
3/4 cup sugar
2 teaspoons baking powder
1/4 teaspoon salt
1 egg, beaten, or 1/4 cup liquid
   egg substitute
1/2 cup skim milk

1/4 cup nonfat sour cream
1/4 cup margarine, softened
1 cup fresh or frozen blueberries
STREUSEL:
1/2 cup sugar
1/3 cup all-purpose flour
2 tablespoons cold margarine
2 tablespoons chopped pecans

1. Preheat oven to 375°.

2. Spray a 9-inch square baking pan with cooking spray.

3. In a large mixing bowl combine flour, sugar, baking powder, and salt. Add egg, milk, sour cream, and margarine; beat well.

4. Fold in blueberries and spread in prepared pan.

5. In another small bowl, combine sugar and flour; cut in margarine until crumbly. Stir in pecans. Sprinkle over batter.

6. Bake for 35 to 40 minutes or until toothpick comes out clean.

Calories per serving: 181 – Fat: 7 g. – Sodium: 203 mg.
For exchange diets, count: 1 1/2 starch, 1 fat.
Preparation time: 20 minutes. – Baking time: 40 minutes.

Used with permission of the innkeepers at Bay Avenue's Sunset Bed & Breakfast

JEWISH SOUR CREAM COFFEE CAKE

24 squares

TOPPING:
1 cup sugar
2 tablespoons cinnamon
1/4 cup chopped pecans
BATTER:
1 1/2 cups sugar
1/2 cup soft margarine

1/2 cup applesauce
1/2 teaspoon salt
2 teaspoons vanilla
4 eggs or 1 cup liquid egg substitute
2 cups nonfat sour cream
3 cups flour
2 teaspoons baking soda

1. Preheat oven to 350°. Spray a 9 x 13-inch baking pan with nonstick cooking spray.

2. In a small bowl, mix sugar, cinnamon, and nuts together and set aside.

3. In a large mixing bowl, cream sugar, margarine, and applesauce. Add salt and vanilla. Beat in eggs. Slowly add the sour cream. Fold in flour and baking soda.

4. Spread half of the batter in the prepared pan. Sprinkle half of the topping over the batter. Add the rest of the batter, followed with the rest of the topping. Cut through the batter with a knife to swirl.

5. Bake for 50 minutes or until cake tests done with toothpick.

Calories per serving: 208 – Fat: 4 g. – Sodium: 195 mg.
For exchange diets, count: 2 starch, 1 fat.
Preparation time: 20 minutes. – Baking time: 50 minutes.

Used with permission of the innkeeper at Calmar Guesthouse

Calmar Guesthouse

Lucille Kruse, Innkeeper
103 West North Street
P.O. Box 206
Calmar, Iowa 52132
(319) 562-3851
www.travelassist.com/reg/ia102s.html

This beautiful restored 1885 Victorian home was built with stained glass windows, open stairway, and gleaming woodwork. Near the world famous hand-carved Bily Brothers Clocks in Spillville and the U.S.-Norwegian Museum in Decorah, the Guesthouse has been home to travelers from all over the world. Lucille has lived out the words of a poem that she learned as a child, "To live in a house by the side of the road and be a friend to man..." by Samuel Walker Foss.

JUDY'S CHEESE COFFEE CAKE
12 wedges

4 ounces reduced-fat cream cheese, softened
4 ounces nonfat cream cheese, softened
1/2 cup sugar
1 tablespoon flour
1 egg or 1/4 cup liquid egg substitute
1 teaspoon vanilla
2 tablespoons nonfat sour cream
1 package refrigerated biscuits
2 tablespoons fruit jam
1 1/2 teaspoons sugar
1/2 teaspoon cinnamon

1. Preheat oven to 350°.

2. Blend first seven ingredients in a mixing bowl with an electric mixer until smooth.

3. Place biscuit dough into deep 10-inch pie pan—press over bottom and up sides of pan. Spread jam over dough. Pour cheese mixture over jam. Sprinkle with sugar and cinnamon.

4. Bake for 26 to 27 minutes until filling is set and crust is brown. Refrigerate any leftovers.

Calories per serving: 188 – Fat: 5 g. – Sodium: 297 mg.
For exchange diets, count: 1 1/2 starch, 1/2 skim milk, 1/2 fat.
Preparation time: 15 minutes. – Baking time: 26 to 27 minutes.

Used with permission of the innkeepers at Charleston Guest House

Charleston Guest House

Judy & Bill Schultz, Innkeepers
612 West Main Street
St. Charles, Illinois 60174
(708) 377-1277

Experience St. Charles' first, and only, bed and breakfast, conveniently located within walking distance of many St. Charles attractions. These attractions include numerous antique shops, great bike trails along the Fox River, many restaurants, nearby parks, the Kane County flea market, and Pheasant Run Convention Center's activities and theatre. This Queen Anne-style home, built in 1892, has three comfortable guest rooms. Guests often request the recipe for this warm cheesecake.

LOW-FAT CINNAMON BREAKFAST CAKE

12 squares

nonstick cooking spray
3/4 cup sugar
1/4 cup no-added-sugar applesauce
1 egg or 1/4 cup liquid egg substitute
1/2 cup skim milk
1 1/2 cups flour
2 teaspoons baking power

1/2 teaspoon salt

STREUSEL TOPPING:
1/3 cup brown sugar
2 tablespoons flour
2 teaspoons cinnamon
2 tablespoons reduced-fat margarine

1. Preheat oven to 350°.

2. Spray a 9-inch square pan with nonstick cooking spray.

3. Combine sugar, applesauce, egg, and milk in a mixing bowl.

4. Add flour, baking powder, and salt. Stir until smooth.

5. In a small mixing bowl, combine ingredients for streusel topping.

6. Pour half of batter into prepared pan. Sprinkle half of streusel topping over batter. Top with remaining batter and top again with streusel.

7. Bake for 30 minutes. Serve warm from the oven.

Suggestion: For a delicious fruit variation, layer 1 cup of finely diced fruit (pear, apple, peach, raspberry) between batter on the bottom and first streusel layer.

Calories per serving: 156 – Fat: 2 g. – Sodium: 188 mg.
For exchange diets, count: 2 starch.
Preparation time: 15 minutes. – Baking time: 30 minutes.

Used with permission of the innkeepers at Bauer Haus Bed & Breakfast (see page 34)

FRESH RHUBARB JAM

48 2-tablespoon servings

5 cups diced fresh rhubarb
4 cups sugar

3-ounce package sugar-free black cherry or raspberry gelatin

1. Boil rhubarb and sugar together in a medium saucepan for 5 minutes. Remove from heat and stir in gelatin.

2. Pour into jelly jars; cover and refrigerate.

Calories per serving: 67 – Fat: 0 – Sodium: 2 mg.
For exchange diets, count: 1 fruit.
Preparation time: 10 minutes.

Used with permission of the innkeepers at Old Brewery Bed and Breakfast (see page 47)

Pennsylvania Dutch Crumb Coffee Cake

12 squares

nonstick cooking spray
1 1/2 cups unsifted flour
1 teaspoon baking powder
1/4 cup shortening
1/4 teaspoon salt
3/4 cup granulated sugar

1 egg or 1/4 cup liquid egg substitute
3/4 cup buttermilk
1/2 teaspoon baking soda
1/4 cup brown sugar
1/4 cup coconut
1 teaspoon cinnamon

1. Preheat oven to 350°. Spray 9-inch square baking pan with nonstick cooking spray.

2. Blend flour, baking powder, shortening, salt, and sugar together. Set aside 1 cup of this mixture as a topping base for use later.

3. In separate bowl, mix the egg, buttermilk, and baking soda together. Then blend in the crumb mixture, stirring thoroughly. There will be some small lumps in the batter. Pour into prepared pan.

4. Add brown sugar, coconut, and cinnamon to the reserved crumb topping. Sprinkle topping on batter.

5. Bake for 35 minutes.

Calories per serving: 172 – Fat: 5 g. – Sodium: 199 mg.
For exchange diets, count: 1 1/2 starch, 1 fat.
Preparation time: 20 minutes. – Baking time: 35 minutes

Used with permission of the innkeeper at Bechtel Victorian Mansion Bed & Breakfast Inn

Bechtel Victorian Mansion Bed & Breakfast Inn

**Charles & Mariam Bechtel and
Ruth Spangler, Innkeepers
400 West King Street
East Berlin, Pennsylvania 17316
(717) 259-7760; Toll free: (800) 530-1108**

Located 18 miles east of Gettysburg, in the East Berlin, Pennsylvania, National Historic District, the Bechtel Victorian Mansion Bed & Breakfast Inn is living proof of lifestyle in the late 19th century. Upon entering the Victorian parlor, one is transplanted back in time, complete with cherry woodwork, gold picture rails, and the original 1897 wallpaper.

LEMON CREAM SCONES

12 scones

nonstick cooking spray
2 cups flour
1/4 cup sugar
2 teaspoons baking powder
rind of one lemon, finely grated

1/4 cup margarine
1/2 cup evaporated skim milk
1 egg or 1/4 cup liquid egg substitute
1 1/2 teaspoons vanilla

1. Preheat oven to 400°.

2. Spray a cookie sheet with cooking spray.

3. Stir together flour, sugar, baking powder, and lemon rind. Cut in margarine until mixture resembles coarse crumbs.

4. In small bowl, mix milk, egg, and vanilla. Add to flour mixture. Knead the dough 10 to 12 times; it will be sticky.

5. Pat dough to 1/2-inch thickness. Cut with a small round glass. Place scones on cookie sheet.

6. Bake for 10 to 15 minutes.

Calories per serving: 132 – Fat: 4 g. – Sodium: 61 mg.
For exchange diets, count: 1 starch, 1 fat.
Preparation time: 20 minutes. – Baking time: 15 minutes.

Used with permission of the innkeepers at The Inn at One Main Street

The Inn at One Main Street

Karen Hart & Mari Zylinski, Innkeepers
One Main Street
Falmouth, Massachusetts 02540
(508) 540-7469; Toll free: (888) 281-6246

Built in 1892 by the Swift family, who were well-known local merchants, this decorative shingled Victorian inn with Queen Anne accents, an open front porch, and a two-story turret offers guests a charming respite in the 300-year-old village of Falmouth. At the Inn at One Main Street, guests wake up to a full gourmet breakfast served in the cheerful dining room with tasty specialties such as gingerbread pancakes topped with fresh whipped cream, cheesy egg puffs, or Cape Cod cranberry pecan waffles. Plenty of freshly brewed coffee, teas, chilled juices, fresh fruits, and a variety of homemade scones or muffins complete the gastronomical extravaganza.

PLUM COFFEE CAKE

24 squares

nonstick cooking spray
1 cup sugar
1/4 cup canola oil
1/4 cup nonfat sour cream
2 eggs or 1/2 cup liquid egg substitute
1 cup buttermilk
3 cups all-purpose flour
1 teaspoon salt

1 tablespoon baking powder
6-8 fresh plums, pitted and sliced
TOPPING:
1/2 cup brown sugar, packed
3 tablespoons all-purpose flour
1 1/2 teaspoons cinnamon
2 tablespoons margarine
2 tablespoons chopped walnuts

1. Preheat oven to 350°. Spray a 9 x 13-inch pan with cooking spray.

2. In mixing bowl, cream sugar, oil, sour cream, and eggs until fluffy. Stir in the buttermilk.

3. In another bowl, sift together the flour, salt, and baking powder. Beat into egg and sugar mixture.

4. Spread batter into prepared pan. Top with rows of plum slices. Combine ingredients for topping, and mix until crumbly. Sprinkle crumbs over plums.

5. Bake approximately 1 hour or until tested done. Cut into 24 squares and serve warm.

Calories per serving: 160 – Fat: 4 g. – Sodium: 191 mg.
For exchange diets, count: 1 starch, 1 fruit, 1/2 fat.
Preparation time: 20 minutes. – Baking time: 1 hour.

Used with permission of the innkeepers at Old Thyme Inn Bed & Breakfast (see page 63)

Sherwood Forest B & B

Keith & Susan Charak, Innkeepers
938 Center Street
P.O. Box 315
Saugatuck, Michigan 49453
(616) 857-1246;
Toll free: (800) 838-1246;
Fax: (616) 857-1996

Experience this beautiful Victorian home, which offers inviting elegance in a wooded setting. Hardwood floors, leaded-glass windows, and the wrap-around porch add to the ideal surroundings. Breakfast is served each morning, featuring such favorites as pecan streusel coffee cake, orange French toast, or potato quiche. During the summer guests can swim in the heated pool or walk 1/2 block to a Lake Michigan public beach to enjoy spectacular sunsets.

Window on the Winds

Leanne McClain, Innkeeper
10151 Highway 191
P.O. Box 996
Pinedale, Wyoming 82941
(307) 367-2600;
Toll free: (888) 367-1345;
Fax: (307) 367-2395
E-mail: lmcclain@wyoming.com

Window on the Winds Bed & Breakfast is located at the base of the Wind River Mountains. These mountains are locally referred to as "the Winds." They offer opportunities for all mountain adventures imaginable, both summer and winter. Leanne serves a healthy, full breakfast featuring a dish or two from the oven and fresh fruit. Her homemade Swiss-style muesli and yogurt, along with pitchers of juice, coffee, and tea are also readily available. With advance notice, Leanne prepares gourmet vegetarian dinners, which can be hard to find in Wyoming.

MCCLAIN'S SCONES

12 1-scone servings

2 cups flour
2 tablespoons sugar
2 teaspoons baking powder
1/4 teaspoon cinnamon
4 tablespoons margarine
1/2 cup dried currants

2 tablespoons nonfat sour cream
1/2 cup skim milk
1/4 cup maple syrup
1 shot scotch
1 egg or 1/4 liquid egg substitute

1. Preheat oven to 425°.

2. Mix flour, sugar, baking powder, and cinnamon. Cut in margarine until the dough resembles fine crumbs. Add currants.

3. Combine sour cream, milk, syrup, scotch, and egg. Mix well. Add to dry ingredients, and knead gently to form a nice biscuit dough.

4. Divide dough in half, and pat each ball into a circle about 1-inch thick. Cut each circle into 6 pie-shape wedges. Place wedges on an ungreased baking sheet.

5. Bake for 15 minutes.

Calories per serving: 145 – Fat: 4 g. – Sodium: 65 mg.
For exchange diets, count: 2 starch.
Preparation time: 20 minutes. – Baking time: 15 minutes.

Used with permission of the innkeeper at Window on the Winds

OATMEAL SCONES

18 scones

1 3/4 cups flour
1 1/2 teaspoons baking powder
3/4 teaspoon baking soda
1/2 teaspoon salt
1/3 cup sugar
1/3 cup soft margarine

1 1/3 cups old-fashioned rolled oats
1/2 cup dried currants
2/3 cup buttermilk
1 egg, beaten lightly, or 1/4 cup liquid
egg substitute

1. Preheat oven to 375°.

2. In a large mixing bowl, thoroughly combine flour, baking powder, baking soda, salt, and sugar. Add margarine and blend until it resembles coarse meal. Mix in oats, currants, and buttermilk until it just forms a sticky dough.

3. On a floured surface knead dough gently six times and roll out into a 1-inch thick round. Cut out rounds with a 3-inch round cutter dipped in flour; transfer to a lightly greased baking sheet.

4. Brush scones with beaten egg and bake for 20 minutes, or until golden brown.

Calories per serving: 124 – Fat: 4 g. – Sodium: 151 mg.
For exchange diets, count: 1 1/2 starch.
Preparation time: 20 minutes. – Baking time: 20 minutes.

Used with permission of the innkeepers at Whispering Pines Bed & Breakfast on Atwood Lake

Whispering Pines Bed & Breakfast on Atwood Lake

Bill & Linda Horn, Innkeepers
P.O. Box 340, State Route 542
Dellroy, Ohio 44620
(330) 735-2824; Fax: (330) 735-7006

Nestled on a gentle slope between century pines and rolling hills lies Whispering Pines Bed & Breakfast. Each of the five guest rooms features fine quality Victorian antiques, private baths, and fabulous lake views. Breakfast consists of a wonderful blend of gourmet coffee, home-baked goods, and an ever-changing menu of delicious specialized entrées. In the warm months breakfast is served on the screen-enclosed wraparound porch overlooking Atwood Lake. When it is cold, breakfast is served in the large gathering room with a roaring fire as background music. Guests may also dine in the evening at Whispering Pines.

Pancakes, Waffles, and French Toast

Citrus Pancakes

4 servings, 2 large pancakes each

2 cups reduced-fat buttermilk
 baking mix
1/2 cup skim milk
1/2 cup fresh-squeezed orange juice

1 egg or 1/4 cup liquid egg substitute
Garnish: drained mandarin oranges

1. Combine all ingredients in a medium mixing bowl, stirring with a whisk.

2. Generously spray an electric griddle with nonstick cooking spray and preheat to 400°.

3. Ladle a generous 1/3 cup of batter onto preheated griddle. Turn pancakes when bubbles appear on the top. Brown second side.

4. Serve with mandarin oranges and syrup.

Calories per serving: 263 – Fat: 4 g. – Sodium: 703 mg.
For exchange diets, count: 3 starch, 1/2 fruit.
Preparation time: 15 minutes.

Used with permission of the innkeepers at Pineapple Hill Bed & Breakfast (see page 38)

Delicate Fluffy Pancakes

6 servings, 3 pancakes each

3 eggs, separated
1 2/3 cups fresh buttermilk
 (do not substitute)
1 teaspoon soda

1 1/2 cups flour
1 tablespoon sugar
1/2 teaspoon salt
1/2 teaspoon butter-flavored extract

1. Separate eggs over a custard cup. Pour whites into a clean mixing bowl; place yolks in a small mixing bowl. Set whites aside and beat yolks well with a rotary beater.

2. Beat in buttermilk and soda.

3. Sift together flour, sugar, and salt. Add to egg and buttermilk and beat well. Stir in butter flavoring.

4. Beat egg whites until stiff; gently fold into other ingredients.

5. Cook on hot griddle, flipping pancakes when bubbles appear.

Variations: Blueberries, diced peaches, or bananas may be sprinkled on the pancakes on the griddle just before flipping. Serve immediately to maintain fluffy texture and flavor.

Calories per serving: 160 – Fat: 3 g. – Sodium: 426 mg.
For exchange diets, count: 2 starch.
Preparation time: 15 minutes.

*Used with permission of the innkeepers at 1874 Stonehouse Bed & Breakfast
on Mulberry Hill (see page 62)*

The Schell Haus Bed & Breakfast

Sharon & Jim Mahanes, Innkeepers
117 Hiawatha Trail
Scenic Highway 11
Pickens, South Carolina 29671
(864) 878-0078; Fax: (864) 878-0066

The Schell Haus is a Victorian-style home tucked away in the foothills of the Blue Ridge Mountains. This perfect getaway for vacations, romantic adventures, and business retreats is situated in the Oolenoy Valley, once the home of the Cherokee Indian. Pumpkintown was the hub of the settler and Indian activities in the late 1700s. Picnic and backpack lunches are available by request in advance.

GERMAN POTATO PANCAKES
10 servings, 2 pancakes + 2 tablespoons syrup each

1/2 cup flour
1 teaspoon salt
1 tablespoon sugar
1 teaspoon baking powder
3 eggs or 3/4 cup liquid egg substitute
1/2 cup skim milk
3 cups coarsely grated potatoes

SWEET AND SOUR SYRUP:
2 cups sugar
1 cup water
1/2 teaspoon maple flavoring
1 tablespoon cider vinegar

1. Combine first 4 ingredients for pancakes in a bowl. Add eggs, milk, and potatoes and beat smooth. Cook on griddle over medium heat until medium brown. Turn to brown both sides.

2. Meanwhile, boil sugar and water for 1 minute, then stir in maple flavoring and cider vinegar.

3. Serve hot pancakes with hot syrup.

Calories per serving: 231 – Fat: 1 g. – Sodium: 303 mg.
For exchange diets, count: 2 starch, 1 fruit.
Preparation time: 15 minutes. Cooking time: 20 minutes.

Used with permission of the innkeepers at Eagles' Landing Bed and Breakfast (see page 52)

GINGER OAT CAKES
6 servings, 2 pancakes each

nonstick cooking spray
1 1/2 cups skim milk
3/4 cup quick oatmeal
1 cup flour
1 1/2 teaspoons baking powder
1 teaspoon ground cinnamon

1/2 teaspoon ground ginger
1/4 teaspoon baking soda
1/4 cup liquid egg substitute
3 egg whites, beaten
1/4 cup unsweetened applesauce

1. Prepare skillet or griddle by spraying with cooking spray. If using an electric griddle, preheat to 375°.

2. In a medium saucepan, heat milk over low heat just until hot. Stir in oats. Remove from heat and let stand 5 minutes. Use a whisk to blend in flour, baking powder, cinnamon, ginger, and soda.

3. Meanwhile, in a medium bowl, combine egg substitute, beaten egg whites, and applesauce. Fold in oat and flour mixture. (Prepared batter can be refrigerated for up to 2 days.)

4. Pour 1/4 cup batter onto prepared griddle and cook until bubbles appear.

5. Turn pancakes and brown on second side. Serve with all-fruit spread.

Suggestion: For a fruit variation, add 1 cup blueberries to the batter.

Calories per serving: 129 – Fat: 1 g. – Sodium: 225 mg.
For exchange diets, count: 1 1/2 starch.
Preparation time: 20 minutes. – Cooking time: 20 minutes.

Used with permission of the innkeepers at Bauer Haus Bed & Breakfast (see page 34)

LAZY COOK'S PANCAKE
4 servings

3 eggs or 3/4 cup liquid egg
  substitute
1 cup flour
1 cup skim milk
2 pinches nutmeg
1 pinch salt

1 tablespoon melted margarine
lemon juice
powdered sugar
Garnish: sliced strawberries and
  whipped cream

1. Preheat oven to 425°.

2. Spray an 8-inch baking dish with nonstick cooking spray.

3. Mix first five ingredients together in a mixing bowl. Mixture will be lumpy. Pour into prepared dish and dot with melted margarine.

4. Bake for 20 minutes. Brush the crusted edges with lemon juice, and sprinkle with powdered sugar.

5. Fill center cavity of baked pancake with fresh or frozen strawberries and top with whipped cream.

Calories per serving: 200 – Fat: 5 g. – Sodium: 153 mg.
For exchange diets, count: 2 starch, 1 fat.
Preparation time: 15 minutes. – Baking time: 20 minutes.

Used with permission of the innkeepers at Old Brewery Bed and Breakfast (see page 47)

POTATO PANCAKES
6 servings

3 eggs or 3/4 cup liquid egg
   substitute
2 cups grated raw potatoes
1 1/2 tablespoons flour
1 1/4 teaspoons salt
1-3 teaspoons grated onion
nonstick cooking spray

TOPPING:
4 Granny Smith apples, cored, peeled,
   and sliced into rings
1/3 cup brown sugar
3 tablespoons flour
1/4 teaspoon cinnamon
GARNISH: fresh blueberries and/or
   raspberries

1. Beat eggs well in a mixing bowl and stir in potatoes. Mix flour and salt together and fold into eggs. Fold in onion.

2. Generously spray a large skillet or griddle with cooking spray. Spoon potato batter onto hot griddle and form into pancake. Cook over medium heat until browned, then turn and cook on other side.

3. Meanwhile, arrange apple rings in a microwaveable dish. Combine brown sugar, flour, and cinnamon, and spread over apple rings. Microwave on high for 2 to 3 minutes.

4. Place some apple topping on each pancake and garnish with blueberries and/or raspberries. Serve hot.

Calories per serving: 192 – Fat: 1 g. – Sodium: 503 mg.
For exchange diets, count: 2 1/2 starch.
Preparation time: 20 minutes.

Used with permission of the innkeepers at Burlington's Willis Graves House

Burlington's Willis Graves House

Jean & Bob Brames, Innkeepers
5825 Jefferson Street
Burlington, Kentucky 41005
(606) 689-5096 or (606) 344-0665

Relax on this 1 1/2-acre property brimming with small town atmosphere. The home was built by Willis Graves, the Boone County clerk in the 1810s and 1820s. Jean prepares a full country breakfast featuring this winning recipe.

RASPBERRY-RHUBARB PANCAKES
4 batches of dry mix, 4 8-inch pancakes per batch

DRY MIX:
1 cup white flour
1 cup quick-cooking oatmeal
2 cups whole wheat flour
1 tablespoon baking soda
1 tablespoon baking powder
1/2 tablespoon sugar
3/4 teaspoon salt

ADDITIONAL INGREDIENTS:
1 cup nonfat buttermilk
1 tablespoon vegetable oil
1 egg
nonfat sour cream
Raspberry/Rhubarb Preserves (recipe
  below)
powdered sugar

1. Combine dry ingredients for pancakes, stirring well to mix. Store in a covered plastic container.

2. To make pancakes, beat buttermilk, oil, and egg together in a mixing bowl. Add 1 cup of dry mix and mix until smooth.

3. Spray a griddle with nonstick cooking spray. Preheat the griddle.

4. Pour batter in a rectangular shape on the griddle. When bubbles appear, turn the pancakes. When browned on second side, remove to a warm platter.

5. To serve, spread pancakes with sour cream and Raspberry/Rhubarb Preserves. Roll up and dust with powdered sugar.

Calories per 8-inch pancake: 131 — Fat: 2 g. — Sodium: 351 mg.
For exchange diets, count: 1 1/2 starch.
Preparation time: 20 minutes.

RASPBERRY/RHUBARB PRESERVES

1. Make raspberry preserves using Suregell Freezer Jam recipe on Suregell package insert (2 cups mashed raspberries + 4 cups of sugar + 1 box of Suregell).

2. Make rhubarb preserves by mixing 2 parts chopped rhubarb with 1 part sugar. Cook until very thick and then refrigerate in jars.

3. Combine 2 parts raspberry preserves with 1 part rhubarb preserves and keep in the refrigerator.

Used with permission of the innkeepers at House of Hunter

House of Hunter

Jean & Walter Hunter, Innkeepers
813 Southeast Kane
Roseburg, Oregon 97470
(541) 672-2335; Toll-free (800) 540-7704
E-mail: walth@wizzards.net/hunter

This 1900 home glows with Italian charm and hospitality. Restored in 1990, this Victorian home is in a quiet residential neighborhood conveniently located on the edge of historic downtown Roseburg. You'll wake up to coffee or tea plus home-baked goodies outside your door, followed by a full breakfast in the dining room. Raspberry-Rhubarb pancakes are served with apple cinnamon pork sausage.

SCRAMBLED PANCAKES (KAISER SCHMARREN)
6 servings

1 tablespoon margarine	1 cup skim milk
1/4 cup sugar	1/3 cup currants or any seasonal
4 eggs, separated	berry
1 pinch of salt	2 tablespoons ground almonds
2 cups flour	Garnish: cinnamon and sugar

1. Cream margarine and sugar together in a mixing bowl. Beat in egg yolks, salt, flour, milk, fruit, and almonds.

2. In a second mixing bowl, beat egg whites until stiff. Carefully fold into the first mixture.

3. Preheat a cast iron or heavy skillet over medium heat. Cook the pancakes until golden brown. Turn and brown the second side.

4. Chop cooked pancakes into pieces. Sprinkle with cinnamon and sugar and serve with a fruit compote on the side.

Calories per serving: 279 – Fat: 8 g. – Sodium: 119 mg.
For exchange diets, count: 2 starch, 1 fat, 1 fruit.
Preparation time: 15 minutes.

Used with permission of the innkeepers at Flemingsburg House Bed & Breakfast at Sweetwater Farm (see page 6)

The Carlson House Bed and Breakfast

Ruth & Ned Ratekin, Innkeepers
105 Park Street
Swedesburg, Iowa 52652
Telephone/Fax (319) 254-2451
E-mail: r2009@se-iowa.net

Experience the Carlson House, a stately home
in the Swedish-American village of Swedesburg. The Carlson House has
been renovated to provide comfort and ambiance for bed-and-breakfast
guests. A guest sitting room provides comfortable lounging with reading
materials, television, snacks, and refreshing drinks. Following wake-up
coffee or tea, guests are served a full breakfast accented with Swedish fare
in the formal dining room and often visit the nearby Swedish-American
Museum.

SWEDISH OVEN PANCAKE (UGNSPANNKAKA)
Serves 4

2 eggs or 1/2 cup liquid egg substitute
1/2 cup flour
1/2 cup skim milk
pinch of nutmeg

2 tablespoons margarine
2 tablespoons powdered sugar
juice of 1/2 lemon

1. Preheat oven to 425°.

2. Beat eggs well if using whole eggs.

3. Mix beaten eggs or egg substitute, flour, milk, and nutmeg together
in a mixing bowl.

4. Melt margarine in oven-proof 10-inch skillet. Pour batter into skillet with melted margarine. Bake for 15 to 20 minutes.

5. Remove from oven, sprinkle with powdered sugar, and return to
oven briefly for sugar to melt.

6. Remove from oven and sprinkle with lemon juice. Cut pancake into
4 wedges. Serve immediately with a variety of toppings such as lingonberries, applesauce, fresh strawberries, peaches, or fruit preserves.

Calories per serving: 141 – Fat: 4 g. – Sodium: 105 mg.
For exchange diets, count: 1 1/2 starch, 1/2 fat.
Preparation time: 10 minutes. – Baking time: 20 minutes.

Used with permission of the innkeepers at The Carlson House Bed and Breakfast

VICTORIAN DESSERT PANCAKES
4 pancakes

1 cup reduced-fat pancake mix
2 teaspoons sugar
1/2 cup reduced-fat shredded
cheddar cheese
1 egg, beaten, or 1/4 cup liquid
egg substitute

1 tablespoon vegetable oil
1 cup skim milk
nonstick cooking spray
4 tablespoons reduced-fat whipped
topping
1/2 cup diced fresh fruit

1. Combine pancake mix, sugar, and cheese in a mixing bowl.

2. Mix together egg or egg substitute, oil, and milk in a mixing bowl.
Pour into dry ingredients and mix well.

3. Spray griddle with cooking spray. Cook pancakes on hot griddle
until tops are bubbly. Turn once and cook until brown.

4. Top each pancake with whipped cream and roll up. Spoon diced fruit
on top of pancake rolls. Serve with additional hot fruit syrup.

Calories per serving: 313 – Fat: 8 g. – Sodium: 752 mg.
For exchange diets, count: 2 starch, 1 fruit, 1 lean meat, 1 fat.
Preparation time: 20 minutes.

Used with permission of the innkeeper at Victorian Lady Bed & Breakfast

Victorian Lady Bed & Breakfast

402 South Pearl
Paola, Kansas 66071
Toll free: (888) VICLADY;
Fax: (913) 294-6996
E-mail: vladyy@msn.com

Designed by famed Kansas architect George
Washburn and built in 1894, this seven-gable Colonial Revival Victorian
B & B is only 2 blocks from the historic Paola Park Square. Each of the
rooms is authentically decorated by era—1890, 1920, and 1940—and
features reproduction wallpaper with original antiques of the period. The
Victorian Lady is located only minutes from downtown Kansas City, the
Country Club Plaza, and Corporate Woods. Enjoy walking through his-
toric Paola with its community theater and drive-in theater, its 25
antique/specialty shops, soda fountain on the square, and friendly people.
You'll enjoy check-in treats, in-room snacks, and a gourmet breakfast.

OATMEAL NUT WAFFLES
8 waffles

1 1/2 cups whole wheat flour
2 teaspoons baking powder
1/2 teaspoon salt
2 eggs, lightly beaten, or 1/2 cup
    liquid egg substitute
2 cups skim milk

2 tablespoons margarine, melted
2 tablespoons nonfat sour cream
2 tablespoons honey
1 cup quick-cooking oats
2 tablespoons chopped pecans
Garnish: sliced fresh peaches

1. In a mixing bowl, combine flour, baking powder, and salt.

2. In a small mixing bowl, combine eggs, milk, margarine, sour cream, and honey. Stir liquid into dry ingredients and mix well. Fold in oats and nuts.

3. Preheat waffle iron and cook waffles. Garnish with peaches.

Calories per serving: 177 – Fat: 5 g. – Sodium: 205 mg.
For exchange diets, count: 2 starch, 1/2 fat.
Preparation time: 20 minutes. – Cooking time: 20 minutes to cook all waffles.

Used with permission of the innkeepers at Peacock Hill Country Inn

Peacock Hill Country Inn

Walter & Anita Ogilvie, Innkeepers
6994 Giles Hill Road
College Grove, Tennessee 37046
(615) 368-7727 for information;
(800) 327-6663 for reservations

Perched atop a gentle hill on a two-lane road that winds through rolling farmland, Peacock Hill Country Inn welcomes its guests to Tennessee with luxurious accommodations, delightful meals, and accessibility to the shopping, fine dining, and entertainment attractions of Nashville and historic Williamson County.

BLUEBERRY-STUFFED FRENCH TOAST

12 servings, 1 square each

nonstick cooking spray

12 slices homemade-type white bread, cut into 1-inch cubes (no crusts)

8-ounce package cold reduced-fat cream cheese, cut into 1-inch cubes

1 cup blueberries

12 large eggs or 3 cups liquid egg substitute

1/3 cup maple syrup or honey

2 cups skim milk

SAUCE:

1 cup sugar

2 tablespoons cornstarch

1 cup water

1 cup blueberries

1 tablespoon margarine

1. Arrange half of bread cubes in a 9 x 13-inch glass baking dish that has been sprayed with nonstick cooking spray.

2. Scatter cubes of cream cheese over bread. Sprinkle blueberries over cream cheese. Arrange remaining bread crumbs over blueberries.

3. In large bowl, whisk together eggs, syrup, and milk. Pour egg mixture evenly over bread mixture. Cover. Chill overnight.

4. In the morning, preheat oven to 350°.

5. Cover pan with foil that has been sprayed with cooking spray to keep toast from sticking. Place in middle of oven. Bake for 30 minutes. Remove foil. Bake for 30 more minutes, or until puffed and golden.

6. To make sauce: In small saucepan, mix together sugar, cornstarch, and water. Cook over moderate high heat, stirring occasionally, for 5 minutes or until thickened. Stir in 1 cup blueberries. Simmer, stirring occasionally, for 10 minutes, or until berries have burst. Add margarine, stirring until it melts. Serve sauce with French toast.

Calories per serving: 242 – Fat: 7 g. – Sodium: 362 mg.
For exchange diets, count: 1 starch, 1 fruit, 1 fat, 1 lean meat.
Preparation time: 20 minutes. Refrigeration time: overnight. – Baking time: 60 minutes.

Used with permission of the innkeepers at Finnish Heritage Homestead Bed & Breakfast
(see page 127)

BRADFORD FRENCH TOAST
WITH RASPBERRY CREAM SAUCE
6 servings, 2 slices each

1 cup evaporated skim milk
2 large eggs or 1/2 cup liquid
   egg substitute
3 tablespoons water
2 tablespoons sugar
1 tablespoon vanilla
1 teaspoon cinnamon

12 thick (3/4-inch) slices French
   bread
2 cups crushed corn flakes
nonstick cooking spray
confectioners' sugar
Raspberry Cream Sauce (recipe follows)
1/2 pint fresh raspberries

1. In a medium bowl, combine the first six ingredients. Dip the bread slices into the mixture and then coat each slice with cereal.

2. Spray a skillet or griddle with cooking spray. Preheat to 375° and then cook each piece until golden and crisp on both sides.

3. To serve, place two pieces of toast on each plate and sprinkle with confectioners' sugar. Top with Raspberry Cream Sauce and raspberries.

RASPBERRY CREAM SAUCE

1 cup fresh or frozen whole
   raspberries, thawed
1 cup nonfat sour cream or nonfat plain
   yogurt

1/2 teaspoon cinnamon

1. Gently fold ingredients together and serve over French toast.

Calories per serving: 265 – Fat: 2 g. – Sodium: 489 mg.
For exchange diets, count: 2 starch, 1 fruit, 1/2 skim milk.
Preparation time: 20 minutes.

Used with permission of the innkeepers at Rosewood Country Inn

Rosewood Country Inn

**Dick & Lesley Marquis, Innkeepers
67 Pleasant View Road
Bradford, New Hampshire 03221
(603) 938-5253;
Toll free: (800) 938-5273**

The Rosewood Country Inn is nestled on 12 hilltop acres in the charming town of Bradford in the Mount Sunapee Lake region of New Hampshire. Its Early-American tradition is recalled in its bordering stone walls, sunlit porches, and inviting common rooms. Breakfast may be enjoyed on the sunlit porches or before the crackling fire in the dining room. Imagine a breakfast of granola, fresh fruit, yogurt, homemade oversized muffins, and this memorable French toast.

DRUNKEN FRENCH TOAST
(Pain Umbriaggo, Italian for "drunk bread")

6 servings

6 thick slices sourdough bread
6 eggs or 1 1/2 cups liquid
   egg substitute
1 teaspoon rum extract or
   2 tablespoons rum

1/2 teaspoon orange extract
1/2 cup skim milk
1/2 cup orange juice
1 tablespoon sugar

1. Arrange sourdough bread in a large baking dish.

2. In a blender container, combine remaining ingredients and process 15 seconds.

3. Pour milk mixture over the bread and allow to stand at least 10 minutes or up to 12 hours (covered) in the refrigerator.

4. Spray a griddle generously with nonstick cooking spray. Preheat griddle to medium high.

5. Carefully move bread slices to the griddle and cook until golden brown. Turn and cook on second side. Serve immediately with flavored syrup or jam.

Calories per serving: 146 – Fat: 3 g. – Sodium: 236 mg.
For exchange diets, count: 1 starch, 1 fruit.
Preparation time: 10 minutes. – Marinating time: 10 minutes up to 12 hours.
Cooking time: 15 minutes.

Used with permission of the innkeepers at Old Town B & B Inn

Old Town B & B Inn

Leigh & Diane Benson, Innkeepers
1521 Third
Eureka, California 95501
(707) 445-3951;
Toll free: (800) 331-5098;
Fax: (707) 268-0231
E-mail: otb-b@dreamwalkerusa.com

Old Town Bed & Breakfast is an 1871 Greek-Revival delight, newly redecorated with original artwork, antiques, plush carpeting, and period wallpapers throughout. Both parlors have marble fireplaces. The breakfast is a four-course American country delight served with gallons of Leigh's "World's Best Coffee" and Diane's blue ribbon-winning jams and breads (10 blue ribbons at the 1995 Humboldt County Fair). Diane is on the faculty at Humboldt State University in the nursing department. Her specialty is heart-healthy food, since her credentials include: R.N., M.S., M. Ed., and Cardiovascular Clinical Nurse Specialist.

The Ashwood

Bob & Bunny Weinman, Innkeepers
2940 Northwest Ashwood Drive
Corvallis, Oregon 97330
(541) 757-9772; Fax: (541) 758-1202
E-mail: ashwood@proaxis.com
www.moriah.com/ashwood

This bed and breakfast welcomes children and pets. It's located in a quiet neighborhood near a shopping center, a fitness center, and Oregon State University.

ELECTRIC GRIDDLE PUFFED FRENCH TOAST
4 servings

4 large eggs or 1 cup liquid
  egg substitute
2/3 cup milk

1 tablespoon margarine
8 thick slices French bread

1. Beat eggs and milk together in a shallow mixing bowl.

2. Preheat griddle to 200°. Coat griddle with margarine.

3. Dip each bread slice into egg and milk mixture just enough to cover and start to soak into the bread. About half of the mixture should remain in the dipping dish.

4. Set temperature of griddle to 250°.

5. Place bread on griddle and immediately pour remaining egg mixture onto the bread, using care to let egg mix soak into the bread.

6. Set temperature of griddle to 300°. Flip the bread slices when they start to turn light brown.

7. Set the temperature of the griddle to 350°. Cook until both sides are golden brown, flipping as necessary. This method of cooking allows the egg to cook thoroughly clear through the bread while remaining puffy. Turn the griddle temperature to high for 20 seconds just prior to removing the toast, then serve it on warmed plates.

Calories per serving: 230 – Fat: 6 g. – Sodium: 473 mg.
For exchange diets, count: 2 starch, 1 lean meat.
Preparation time: 20 minutes.

Used with permission of the innkeepers at The Ashwood

MAKE AHEAD FRENCH TOAST Á L'ORANGE
4 servings

3 eggs or 3/4 cup liquid egg substitute
1/8 teaspoon orange extract
1/8 teaspoon vanilla extract
1 1/2 cups evaporated skim milk

nonstick cooking spray
4 thick slices French bread
cinnamon
2 thin slices of orange

1. In a medium mixing bowl, beat eggs, extracts, and evaporated skim milk until fully blended.

2. Spray a 9 x 13-inch baking pan with cooking spray. Place French bread in the pan. Pour egg mixture evenly over bread, turning bread several times until liquid is completely absorbed.

3. Sprinkle with cinnamon and place two thin slices of orange on top for garnish.

4. Cover with plastic wrap and refrigerate overnight.

5. Remove plastic and bake at 375° for 25 to 30 minutes or until golden brown. Serve with raspberry-flavored syrup.

Calories per serving: 182 – Fat: 3 g. – Sodium: 367 mg.
For exchange diets, count: 1 starch, 1 skim milk.
Preparation time: 15 minutes. Refrigeration time: overnight. – Baking time: 30 minutes.

Used with permission of the innkeepers at Holly Hedge House Bed & Breakfast

Holly Hedge House Bed & Breakfast

Lynn & Marian Thrasher, Innkeepers
908 Grant Avenue South
Renton, Washington 98055
(206) 226-2555;
Toll free (reservations only): (888) 226-2555
E-mail: holihedg@nwlink.com

Seattle-area visitors can enjoy the "Spirit of Washington Dinner Train Package." This includes a gourmet dinner served while enjoying a picturesque 3 1/2-hour excursion aboard the "Spirit" to Columbia Winery and two nights (minimum) at the Holly Hedge House.

INDIVIDUAL FRENCH TOAST IN THE MICROWAVE

1 serving

nonstick cooking spray
1 3/4-inch slice French bread
1/4 cup liquid egg substitute

1/8 cup skim milk
1/4 teaspoon vanilla
sprinkle of cinnamon and sugar

1. Spray a large (6 ounce) custard cup with nonstick cooking spray.

2. Combine egg substitute, milk, and vanilla in a small mixing bowl.

3. Pour egg mixture over the bread and sprinkle with cinnamon and sugar. Put bread in the custard cup.

4. Microwave on 70 percent power for 2 minutes. Check for doneness. Egg should be set, with no liquid remaining. If not, cook for an additional 30 seconds and check again.

5. Serve with vanilla or maple syrup.

Calories per serving: 122 – Fat: 3 g. – Sodium: 226 mg.
For exchange diets, count: 1 starch, 1 lean meat.
Preparation time: 5 minutes. – Baking time: 2 minutes.

Used with permission of the innkeepers at Glass Door Inn Bed & Breakfast

Glass Door Inn Bed & Breakfast

Linda & Richard Merrick, Innkeepers
R.R. 3, Box 101
Fairfield, Illinois 62837
(618) 847-4512
E-mail: gdinn@midwest.net
www.quickcaps.com/gdi.html

The Glass Door Inn, a newly constructed bed and breakfast with all of today's modern conveniences, is nestled in a serene, rural setting. The Inn, just 2.3 miles from Fairfield, is located on 2 acres of open countryside. Guests can roam the adjoining 70 acres of open fields and trees, encountering a small lake, deer, wildflowers, and nature at its best.

BLUEBERRY WAFFLES
6 waffles

1 1/2 cups reduced-fat pancake
  or baking mix
1 egg or 1/4 cup liquid egg substitute
1 tablespoon vegetable oil

3/4 cup skim milk
1/2 cup reduced-calorie blueberry pie
  filling
nonstick cooking spray

1. Combine baking mix with egg, oil, and milk. Beat until smooth. Carefully fold in pie filling.

2. Spray a waffle iron with cooking spray. Cook waffles and serve with syrup of choice. Keep waffles warm by stacking in a covered cake saver.

Calories per serving: 173 – Fat: 4 g. – Sodium: 371 mg.
For exchange diets, count: 1 fruit, 1 starch, 1 fat.
Preparation time: 15 minutes.

Used with permission of the innkeepers at Old Brewery Bed and Breakfast (see page 47)

LOW-FAT OVEN-BAKED FRENCH TOAST
4 servings, 2 slices each

1/2 cup liquid egg substitute
2 teaspoons vanilla
3/4 cup skim milk
1 teaspoon cinnamon
nonstick cooking spray
8 slices low-fat white or wheat bread

FRUIT SYRUP:
2/3 cup fruit juice
2 tablespoons honey
1 1/2 teaspoons cornstarch
1/8 teaspoon cinnamon

1. Preheat oven to 450°.

2. Combine liquid egg substitute, vanilla, skim milk, and cinnamon in a large bowl.

3. Spray a large cookie sheet thoroughly with cooking spray. Dip bread in liquid, lightly coating each side. Place bread on the cookie sheet and bake for 6 to 8 minutes.

4. Lightly spray the cookie sheet again; turn bread over and brown the other side for 6 to 8 more minutes.

5. Mix together ingredients for fruit syrup in a small saucepan. Cook over medium heat, stirring constantly, about 3 minutes or until thick and bubbly. Serve over warm French toast.

Calories per serving: 228 – Fat: 3 g. – Sodium: 350 mg.
For exchange diets, count: 2 starch, 1 lean meat.
Preparation time: 15 minutes. – Baking time: 15 minutes.

Used with permission of the innkeepers at Glass Door Inn Bed & Breakfast

NEARLY GUILT-FREE PINEAPPLE CHEESE TOAST
12 servings, 1 sandwich each

1 cup low-calorie apricot preserves
1/2 cup low-fat ricotta cheese
8 ounces reduced-fat cream cheese
20-ounce can juice-pack pineapple, drained very well
1 loaf French bread, cut into 3/4-inch slices

1 teaspoon vanilla
1 cup milk
4 eggs, beaten, or 1 cup liquid egg substitute
1/2 teaspoon nutmeg
1 tablespoon sugar

1. Preheat oven to 325°.

2. In a mixing bowl, combine the cheeses, preserves, and pineapple.

3. Generously coat half the bread slices with cheese mixture. Top with the second slice of bread.

4. Combine remaining ingredients in a shallow dish.

5. Generously spray a nonstick skillet or griddle with cooking spray. Preheat to medium heat.

6. Coat each side of the "sandwich" in egg mixture and brown lightly on the griddle.

7. Place browned sandwiches on a foil-lined baking sheet. Bake for 20 minutes. Serve with praline syrup or apricot preserves.

Calories per serving: 223 – Fat: 6 g. – Sodium: 319 mg.
For exchange diets, count: 2 starch, 1 lean meat.
Preparation time: 20 minutes – Baking time: 20 minutes.

Used with permission of the innkeepers at Cameron's Crag Bed & Breakfast (see page 197)

STRAWBERRY SAUCE FOR WAFFLES AND PANCAKES
12 servings, 1/4 cup each

1 quart strawberries, washed, hulled, and sliced
1/2 cup sugar

2 tablespoons cornstarch
1/2 cup water

1. Measure 1 cup of strawberries into a saucepan and mash well.

2. In a small cup, mix sugar and cornstarch together; stir into the berries. Stir in water.

3. Cook over medium heat, stirring constantly, until the mixture thickens and boils. Continue cooking for 1 minute.

4. Cool to room temperature and stir in the remaining berries.

Calories per serving: 56 – Fat: 0 – Sodium: 1 mg.
For exchange diets, count: 1 fruit.
Preparation time: 15 minutes.

Used with permission of the innkeepers at Bauer Haus Bed & Breakfast (see page 34)

Egg Entrées

Briarwold Bed and Breakfast

Marion & Charles Criner, Innkeepers
5400 Lincoln Highway
York, Pennsylvania 17406
(717) 252-4619

The Briarwold Bed and Breakfast is a restored
brick Federal home built circa 1830, situated on three acres of lawn and
trees. There are two Persian kittens, Tulip and Fred, who claim the bed
and breakfast as residence. In the mornings, a full gourmet breakfast is
served in the dining room. Seasonal fresh fruit, home-baked breads and
sweets, and a variety of delicious entrées are served. Dietary restrictions
are accommodated by notifying the hosts in advance.

ALMOND SUPREME OMELET
1 serving

2 eggs or 1/2 cup liquid egg substitute	5 teaspoons Brie cheese
1 tablespoon cold water	2 tablespoons slivered toasted
1 teaspoon baking powder	almonds
1/2 teaspoon margarine	salt and pepper to taste

1. Whip the eggs with the water and baking powder.

2. Melt margarine in an omelet pan; add egg mixture to hot pan, and
use spatula to lift eggs as they cook. Dot Brie evenly over eggs. Add
almonds when cheese melts.

3. Season with salt and pepper, carefully fold in half with spatula, and
serve with crisp bacon and a wedge of ripe tomato.

Calories per serving: 257 – Fat: 17 g. – Sodium: 341 mg.
For exchange diets, count: 3 lean meat, 2 fat.
Preparation time: 15 minutes.

Used with permission of the innkeepers at Briarwold Bed and Breakfast

ASIAGO & ASPARAGUS OMELET
1 serving

3 stalks asparagus	salt and fresh ground pepper to taste
2 eggs or 1/2 cup liquid egg substitute	1 ounce sliced Asiago cheese
2 tablespoons water	pinch of fresh tarragon

1. Chop the asparagus stalks, leaving the tops for ornamentation.
Steam the chopped stalks until tender (about 4 to 8 minutes).

2. Heat nonstick pan that has been brushed with oil. Whisk together
eggs, water, salt, and pepper. Pour egg mixture into pan, swirling
around and lifting gently so that all eggs cook.

3. While eggs are cooking, place the steamed asparagus and cheese on half of the omelet. Sprinkle with tarragon. Gently fold the other half over.

4. Once set, lift and move omelet to serve or keep in warm oven until all omelets are ready. Arrange reserved asparagus tops in a semi-circle and lay a tarragon twig on top.

Bruce offers a tip for freezing asparagus: My mother has a great asparagus patch and she taught me how to freeze them individually. After you clean and blanch the asparagus, spread them on a cookie sheet lined with wax paper and freeze. After they are frozen, you can then place them in a plastic freezer bag. This way, you'll be able to grab a few spears or as many as you like without them all freezing together in a big glob.

Calories per serving: 220 – Fat: 13 g. – Sodium: 487 mg.
For exchange diets, count: 3 lean meat, 1 fat.
Preparation time: 20 minutes.

Used with permission of the innkeepers at The Artist's Inn & Gallery

The Artist's Inn & Gallery

Jan & Bruce Garrabrandt, Innkeepers
117 East Main Street
P.O. Box 26
Terre Hill, Pennsylvania 17581
(717) 445-0219; Fax: (717) 445-0219
E-mail: artistin@postoffice.ptd.net

Spend the night in an art gallery! A 150-year-old Federal-style home, the Artist's Inn & Gallery is located in small town Terre Hill and nestled among Amish and Mennonite farms. Breakfast is a memorable event as all the food is made from scratch and features eggs and produce from nearby farms, flour and grains from a local mill, and even chocolate from a nearby chocolate factory. The meals are served by candlelight and you have a choice of eating in the dinning room or al fresco on the Victorian porch.

CREAMY SCRAMBLED EGGS

4 2/3-cup servings

8 eggs or 2 cups liquid egg substitute
1/4 cup milk
1/4 teaspoon salt
dash of pepper
1 teaspoon margarine

3-ounce package light (50% less fat)
cream cheese with chives, cut into
1/2-inch cubes
chopped parsley (optional)

1. In a medium bowl, beat eggs, milk, salt, and pepper until just combined.

2. Melt margarine in a large skillet over low heat. Pour in egg mixture. Cook over low heat. As eggs begin to set on bottom, gently lift cooked portion with spatula, letting uncooked portion flow to bottom of pan.

3. Drop cream cheese cubes on top of eggs. Cook until eggs are no longer runny and cheese is melted. Sprinkle with chopped parsley, if desired.

Calories per serving: 163 – Fat: 9 g. – Sodium: 357 mg.
For exchange diets count: 2 lean meat, 1 fat.
Preparation time: 15 minutes.

Used with permission of the innkeepers at Sara's Bed & Breakfast Inn

Sara's Bed & Breakfast Inn

Donna & Tillman Arledge, Innkeepers
941 Heights Boulevard
Houston, Texas 77008
(713) 868-1130;
Toll free: (800) 593-1130

Sara's is located in Houston Heights, a neighborhood long recognized for its diversity of turn-of-the-century architectural styles in both residential and commercial buildings. Sara's has 14 bedrooms furnished with antiques and collectibles. Enjoy sitting in the 1,000-square-foot garden room with warm breakfast muffins and a hot cup of tea or coffee or indulge in an afternoon soda on the veranda.

BEST EVER VEGGIE OMELET
1 large omelet, serves 1–2 people

1/4 cup chopped green pepper
1/4 cup chopped tomato
1/4 cup chopped mushrooms
1 tablespoon chopped black olives
1 tablespoon chopped fresh chives

1 teaspoon vegetable oil
3 eggs or 3/4 cup liquid egg substitute
1/4 cup shredded reduced-fat cheddar
   or American cheese

1. Prepare vegetables and set aside. Preheat 8-inch skillet over medium heat, spreading oil over bottom and sides of skillet.

2. In a medium bowl, whip eggs or egg substitute for 1 minute.

3. Pour eggs into skillet and roll egg around to the edges of the skillet several times to build up the outside edge of the omelet.

4. Sprinkle prepared vegetables, olives, and chives over one side of the omelet. Add cheese and cook until egg is firm. Fold omelet in half, and gently remove to a preheated serving plate.

Calories per recipe: 325 – Fat: 18 g. – Sodium: 854 mg.
For exchange diets, count: 3 lean meat, 2 vegetable, 2 fat.
Preparation time: 15 minutes.

Used with permission of the innkeepers at Old Brewery Bed and Breakfast (see page 47)

DILLED EGGS WITH SALMON
4 3/4-cup servings

8 eggs or 2 cups liquid egg substitute
2 tablespoons cold water
6 drops hot sauce

4 ounces 50% reduced-fat cream
   cheese
2 ounces smoked salmon
1 teaspoon fresh dill

1. Scramble eggs with water and hot sauce over medium heat in a non-stick skillet.

2. Cut cream cheese into pieces. Dice salmon into 1/2-inch pieces. Snip dill.

3. When eggs are no longer liquid, add cream cheese and salmon. Add dill at end of cooking.

Calories per serving: 166 – Fat: 8 g. – Sodium: 451 mg.
For exchange diets, count: 3 lean meat.
Preparation time: 15 minutes.

Used with permission of the innkeeper at Old Town B & B Inn (see page 97)

POTATO OMELET
4 servings

1 potato, unpeeled
1 tablespoon olive oil
1 medium onion, sliced thin
1 teaspoon minced garlic

6 eggs, well beaten, or 1 1/2 cups
  liquid egg substitute
4-ounce can chopped green chiles

1. Preheat oven to 350°.

2. Poke the potato with a fork several times, and microwave on high power for 5 minutes or until tender. Cut the potato into thin slices.

3. In an 8-inch oven-proof skillet, sauté onion and garlic in olive oil for 3 minutes.

4. Remove from heat, pour eggs into the skillet, and sprinkle chiles and potato slices on top.

5. Bake for 10 to 12 minutes or until the egg is well set. Use a spatula to carefully fold omelet in half. Cut into 4 wedges and serve.

Calories per serving: 175 – Fat: 6 g. – Sodium: 171 mg.
For exchange diets, count: 1 starch, 1 lean meat, 1 fat.
Preparation time: 15 minutes. – Baking time: 12 minutes.

Used with permission of the innkeepers at Bauer Haus Bed & Breakfast (see page 34)

Casa de Patron B and B Inn

Jeremy & Cleis Jordan, Innkeepers
P.O. Box 27
Lincoln, New Mexico 88338
(505) 653-4676; Toll free: (800) 524-5202;
Fax: (505) 653-4671
E-mail: patron@pvtnetworks.net
www.casapatron.com

Driving down a quiet country road into a wonderfully preserved territorial village, you will come upon a thick-walled adobe hacienda called Casa de Patron. This historic bed & breakfast was once the home of Juan Patron, the youngest speaker of the house in the early New Mexican Territorial Legislature. Pull in your reins here for a good night's sleep with the fresh smell of sun-dried linens, as did our most famous houseguest, Billy the Kid. Start your morning with an invigorating stroll in the fresh mountain air, returning to the aromas of a hearty country breakfast and often music by the hostess on the resident pipe organ.

FEATHERBED EGGS
12 squares

nonstick cooking spray
2 cups French bread cut into small cubes
  or crumbled cornbread
1/4 teaspoon salt
1/4 teaspoon black pepper
4 ounces reduced-fat sharp cheddar
  cheese, shredded

4 ounces reduced-fat Monterey Jack
  cheese, shredded
10 large eggs or 2 1/2 cups liquid
  egg substitute
2 cups skim milk
1 teaspoon basil
1 teaspoon marjoram

1. Preheat oven to 350°. Spray a 14 or 15 x 11-inch shallow glass baking dish with cooking spray.

2. Spread French bread cubes in an even layer in the prepared dish. Sprinkle lightly with salt and pepper. Evenly distribute the cheese over the bread.

3. Whisk the eggs, milk, and seasonings together until blended. Pour egg mixture over the bread and cheese.

4. Bake in oven until the eggs are set and the top is very lightly browned and slightly puffed, about 30 to 35 minutes. Do not overbake.

Recipe can be prepared the night before, covered and refrigerated, and baked in the morning.

Calories per serving: 141 – Fat: 5 g. – Sodium: 303 mg.
For exchange diets, count: 2 lean meat, 1/2 starch.
Preparation time: 15 minutes. – Baking time: 35 minutes.

Used with permission of the innkeepers at Old Thyme Inn Bed & Breakfast (see page 63)

BREAKFAST PIE
6 servings

nonstick cooking spray
1/2 cup chopped onion
1/2 cup chopped zucchini
2 ounces cooked mushrooms
2 ounces lean ham
1/2 cup shredded reduced-fat
  cheddar cheese

1 cup skim milk
2 tablespoons nonfat sour cream
2 eggs or 1/2 cup liquid egg substitute
  or 3 egg whites
3/4 cup reduced-fat buttermilk baking
  mix
pinch pepper

1. Preheat oven to 350°.

2. Spray 9-inch pie plate with cooking spray.

3. Spray skillet with cooking spray; add onion, zucchini, mushrooms, and ham. Cook about 2 minutes until onions are translucent.

4. Spread onion mixture over bottom of pie plate. Sprinkle cheese on top.

5. In bowl, combine the rest of the ingredients and blend with fork. Pour into pie plate. Bake until golden brown and puffy, about 35 to 45 minutes. Cut into 6 wedges and serve.

Calories per serving: 180 – Fat: 5 g. – Sodium: 424 mg.
For exchange diets, count: 1 starch, 1 vegetable, 1 medium-fat meat.
Preparation time: 15 minutes. – Baking time: 45 minutes.

Used with permission of the innkeepers at Pineapple Hill Bed & Breakfast (see page 38)

Joy's Morning Glory Bed and Breakfast

Merle & Joy Petersen, Innkeepers
4308 Main Street
Elk Horn, Iowa 51531
(712) 764-5631

Staying at this B & B is like stepping back to Denmark in 1912. Guests enjoy an abundant array of flowers that line the walkways and a comfortable rocker on the front porch. This inn is in the heart of America's largest rural Danish settlement with antiques, Danish foods, a Danish windmill, and the Danish Immigrant Museum nearby. This recipe was enjoyed by Iowa Governor Terry Branstad on his visit to the inn.

CRUSTLESS HAM AND EGG QUICHE
6 servings

nonstick cooking spray
1 2/3 cups skim milk
1/2 cup reduced-fat baking mix
3 eggs or 3/4 cup liquid egg substitute

1 tablespoon margarine, melted
dash of pepper
3 ounces lean ham, cubed
3 ounces reduced-fat cheese, shredded

1. Preheat oven to 350°.

2. Spray a 9-inch pie pan with cooking spray.

3. In a blender container, combine milk, baking mix, eggs, margarine, and pepper. Blend for 15 seconds.

4. Pour into prepared pan and sprinkle with ham and cheese. Gently press ham and cheese under the egg mixture.

5. Bake for 30 minutes or until a knife inserted halfway between the center and edge comes out clean. Let stand 10 minutes before serving.

Calories per slice: 161 – Fat: 6 g. – Sodium: 452 mg.
For exchange diets, count: 1/2 starch, 2 lean meat.
Preparation time: 15 minutes. – Baking time: 30 minutes.
Cooling time: 10 minutes.

Used with permission of the innkeepers at Joy's Morning Glory Bed and Breakfast

COUNTRY BREAKFAST PIE

8 slices

1/2 pound reduced-fat spicy pork sausage

2 ounces grated reduced-fat Swiss cheese

9-inch pie shell, unbaked

4 eggs, lightly beaten, or 1 cup liquid egg substitute

1/4 cup chopped green pepper

1/4 cup chopped red pepper

3-ounce can chopped green chiles, drained (optional)

2 tablespoons chopped onion

1 cup evaporated skim milk

1. Preheat oven to 375°.

2. Crumble and cook sausage until done. Drain well.

3. Mix cheese and sausage and put in pie shell.

4. Combine eggs with remaining ingredients. Pour into shell. Sprinkle top with additional red and green pepper if desired for garnish.

5. Bake for 40 to 45 minutes. Cool 5 to 10 minutes before cutting into 6 or 8 slices.

Calories per serving: 223 – Fat: 11 g. – Sodium: 225 mg.
For exchange diets, count: 1 starch, 2 lean meat, 1 fat.
Preparation time: 20 minutes. – Baking time: 45 minutes.
Cooling time: 10 minutes.

Used with permission of the innkeepers at Gaines Landing Bed & Breakfast

Gaines Landing Bed & Breakfast

Darlene & Ted Barber, Innkeepers
521 West Atlantic
Branson, Missouri 65616
(417) 334-2280 (information);
Toll free: (800) 825-3145 (reservations)
E-mail: darlene@tri-lakes.net
http://bransoninfo.com/gaines/landing.htm

Experience a contemporary home located in a quiet wooded oasis within walking distance of historic downtown Branson and Lake Taneycomo. Features include an outdoor hot tub for each guest room. The common area includes a swimming pool, wet bar, refrigerator, microwave, and coffeepot. Each room is cheerfully decorated and includes king or queen bed, private bath, and TV. Gaines Landing Bed & Breakfast is only one block from the famous Branson Strip. A friend gave the innkeeper this recipe when they started the inn.

GREEN CHILE QUICHE

8 servings

nonstick cooking spray
4 ounces (or 1 cup shredded) grated
    reduced-fat pepper Jack cheese
1 small can chopped green chiles
2 teaspoons cumin
2 tablespoons dried cilantro

1 teaspoon black pepper
1 tomato, chopped
6 eggs or 1 1/2 cups liquid egg
    substitute
3 cups skim milk
1 1/2 cups reduced-fat baking mix

1. Preheat oven to 375°.

2. Spray a quiche dish with cooking spray.

3. In a medium mixing bowl, mix together cheese, chiles, seasonings, and tomato. Spoon this mixture into prepared quiche pan.

4. In a large bowl, mix together eggs or egg substitute, milk, and baking mix. Pour over the cheeses and tomatoes.

5. Garnish the top with additional dried cilantro and cumin.

6. Bake for 40 minutes or until quiche tests done.

Calories per serving: 202 – Fat: 5 g. – Sodium: 445 mg.
For exchange diets, count: 1 1/2 lean meat, 1/2 skim milk, 1 starch.
Preparation time: 10 minutes. – Baking time: 40 minutes.

Used with permission of the innkeeper at Eagle River Inn

Eagle River Inn

Patty Bidez, Innkeeper
145 North Main Street
P.O. Box 100
Minturn, Colorado 81645
Toll free: (800) 344-1750;
Fax: (970) 827-4020
E-mail: eri@vail.net

Eagle River is a 103-year-old inn in the Rocky Mountains, located just around the bend from Vail and Beaver Creek Resorts. Guests enjoy the hot tub overlooking the Eagle River plus complimentary wine and appetizers each evening.

GARDEN POLENTA PIE
2 pies, 6 slices each

nonstick cooking spray
1 cup polenta
3 cups water
1/3 cup grated Parmesan cheese
1 teaspoon salt
1 1/2 cups thinly sliced zucchini
2 cups thinly sliced mushrooms
1/2 cup chopped sun-dried tomatoes
1 cup diced green onions

Mrs. Dash to taste
6 eggs, beaten, or 1 1/2 cups liquid
  egg substitute
1 cup low-fat cottage cheese
4 ounces grated reduced-fat pepper
  Jack cheese
2 cups skim milk

2 tablespoons grated Parmesan cheese

1. Preheat oven to 350°.

2. Spray two pie plates with cooking spray.

3. To make crust, combine polenta and water in a saucepan; bring to a boil. Stir until it begins to thicken. Remove from heat and stir in Parmesan cheese and salt. Spread over bottom of pie plates.

4. Sauté zucchini, mushrooms, tomatoes, and green onions in a skillet over medium heat until tender.

5. Mix vegetables with remaining ingredients, except the Parmesan cheese, and spread evenly over crusts. Sprinkle with 2 tablespoons Parmesan cheese.

6. Bake for 40 to 45 minutes until lightly browned and center is set.

Note: If you have other vegetables go ahead and add them.

Calories per serving: 168 – Fat: 4 g. – Sodium: 451 mg.
For exchange diets, count: 1 starch, 1 vegetable, 2 very lean meat.
Preparation time: 15 minutes. – Baking time: 45 minutes.

Used with permission of the innkeepers at Joshua Grindle Inn (see page 55)

GUESTHOUSE QUICHE
8 slices

nonstick cooking spray
6 slices white bread
1 cup shredded reduced-fat cheese
of your choice (suggest hot pepper)
1/2 cup cubed cooked lean meat
of your choice (suggest chicken)
1/2 cup vegetables of your choice
(suggest onions, peppers, and
mushrooms)

6 eggs, well beaten, or 1 1/2 cups
liquid egg substitute
1 cup milk
2 tablespoons water
Garnish: chopped fresh herbs such as
basil, oregano, parsley, or cilantro

1. Preheat oven to 375°. Spray a 9-inch pie pan with cooking spray.

2. Line pan with slices of bread, pressing into the corners.

3. Layer cheese, meat, and vegetables over the bread.

4. Mix eggs, milk, and water together in a bowl and pour over the vegetables.

5. Gently press bread down with a fork to ensure it is soaked.

6. Top with chopped fresh herbs, and bake for 40 minutes or until quiche tests done with toothpick.

Calories per serving: 120 – Fat: 3 g. – Sodium: 384 mg.
For exchange diets, count: 1 starch, 1 lean meat.
Preparation time: 15 minutes. – Baking time: 40 minutes.

Used with permission of the innkeeper at Calmar Guesthouse (see page 76)

PESTO SOUFFLÉ
4 servings

nonstick cooking spray
2 ounces reduced-fat Monterey Jack
cheese, shredded
4 large eggs, beaten, or 1 cup
liquid egg substitute
1 1/2 teaspoons Dijon mustard

1 tablespoon pesto
1/2 cup evaporated skim milk
1/2 teaspoon salt
1/4 teaspoon pepper
Garnish: fresh basil and diced tomato

1. Preheat oven to 375°.

2. Spray four ramekins generously with cooking spray and divide cheese among them.

3. In a mixing bowl, whisk together eggs, mustard, pesto, milk, salt, and pepper. Pour egg mixture over the cheese in the ramekins.

4. Bake for 18 to 20 minutes. Garnish with fresh basil leaves and diced tomato before serving.

Calories per serving: 119 – Fat: 4 g. – Sodium: 445 mg.
For exchange diets, count: 2 lean meat.
Preparation time: 10 minutes. – Baking time: 20 minutes.

Used with permission of the innkeepers at Victoria Tyme Inn Bed & Breakfast

Victoria Tyme Inn Bed & Breakfast

Jodie & Jeff Padgett, Innkeepers
511 East First South Street
Carlinville, Illinois 62626
(217) 854-8689;
Fax: (217) 854-5122
E-mail: victyme@accunet.net

Cross the threshold into the elegance of a bygone era and be pampered in old-world ambiance! Located in Carlinville's historic district, the Victoria Tyme Inn was listed on the National Historic Register in 1976 for its architectural significance. The inn is actually composed of two distinct houses built on the property, one circa 1857 and the other circa 1876, which were later joined. The antebellum house was the birthplace and early childhood home of Mary Hunter Austin, a pioneering naturalist, feminist, and famed author of the American Southwest.

Benson Bed & Breakfast

Stan & Norma Anderson, Innkeepers
402 North Oakland Avenue
Oakland, Nebraska 68045-1135
(402) 685-6051

Experience the Benson Bed & Breakfast, located
in the small Swedish town of Oakland, Nebraska.
The second floor of the Benson Building hosts bed-and-breakfast guests
in its beautiful facilities. You can view Oakland's Main Street from the
delightfully bright and airy Garden Room or purchase crafts and gifts in
the shop on the main floor. Visit the Swedish Heritage Center while you
are there.

QUICHE LORRAINE
8 slices

10-inch pie crust
8 ounces Canadian bacon, diced
4 ounces shredded reduced-fat
 Swiss cheese
4 eggs, beaten, or 1 cup liquid
 egg substitute

2 cups evaporated skim milk
1 tablespoon flour
1/4 teaspoon pepper
1/4 teaspoon nutmeg

1. Preheat the oven to 400°.

2. Bake the pie crust for 3 minutes only. Remove from oven and prick
bottom and sides with a fork. Bake 5 minutes longer. Remove from
oven and cool.

3. Sprinkle Canadian bacon into cooled shell. Add Swiss cheese.

4. In a small bowl, combine all remaining ingredients, stirring well.
Pour over cheese layer. Sprinkle lightly with extra nutmeg.

5. Turn the oven temperature down to 375°, and bake for 45 minutes
or until the middle is set.

Calories per serving: 243 – Fat: 11 g. – Sodium: 617 mg.
For exchange diets, count: 1 lean meat, 1 skim milk, 1 fat, 1/2 starch.
Preparation time: 15 minutes. – Baking time: 8 minutes for crust,
45 minutes for prepared quiche.

Used with permission of the innkeepers at Benson Bed & Breakfast

QUICKIE BLENDER QUICHE
WITH THREE VARIATIONS
6 servings

nonstick cooking spray
4 ounces shredded reduced-fat cheese
4 eggs or 1 cup liquid egg substitute

1 cup reduced-fat buttermilk baking
   mix
2 cups skim milk

1. Preheat oven to 350°.

2. Spray a 10-inch pie pan or quiche pan with cooking spray and spread cheese over bottom.

3. Add one of the following:

   a. 1/2 cup cooked chopped broccoli. Sprinkle with 1/2 teaspoon Tabasco sauce.

   b. 2 ounces diced lean ham and 1 finely chopped green onion

   c. 4 slices bacon, broiled until crisp and crumbled

4. Blend eggs or egg substitute, baking mix, and milk in blender. Pour blended mixture over cheese and other ingredients.

5. Bake for 45 minutes. Filling will puff slightly and be golden brown on top.

Calories per serving (using ham variation): 219 – Fat: 6 g. – Sodium: 649 mg.
For exchange diets, count: 2 1/2 lean meat, 1 starch.
Preparation time: 15 minutes. – Baking time: 45 minutes.

Used with permission of the innkeepers at The Inn at Ludington

The Inn at Ludington

Diane Shields & David Nemitz, Innkeepers
701 East Ludington Avenue
Ludington, Michigan 49431
(616) 845-7055;
Toll-free: (800) 845-9170

Breakfast is an event here, not an afterthought.
Early morning coffee and muffins are followed by a bountiful breakfast buffet, using only the best natural ingredients and real maple syrup. A guest comments: "We like this slightly firmer form of quiche better than the custardy classic."

SOUR CREAM SOUFFLÉ
6 servings

6 large egg yolks
1/2 cup nonfat sour cream
1/4 cup grated Parmesan cheese
1/4 teaspoon salt
6 egg whites, beaten until stiff
1 tablespoon butter-flavored margarine

TOPPING:
1/2 cup nonfat sour cream
2 tablespoons sugar
1 cup fresh raspberries, blueberries,
   or strawberries

1. Preheat oven to 325°.

2. Beat egg yolks till thick and lemon-colored, about 5 minutes. Combine sour cream with Parmesan cheese. Add 1/2 cup of the sour cream mixture to egg yolks, along with the salt; beat. Fold in egg whites.

3. Melt margarine in a 10-inch heavy, ovenproof skillet; pour in egg mixture, leveling gently. Cook over very low heat 10 minutes.

4. Carefully move to oven and bake for 15 minutes until golden and puffed.

5. Meanwhile, mix sour cream and sugar together. Cut the soufflé into 6 wedges. Serve with a dollop of the sweetened sour cream and top with berries.

Calories per serving: 169 – Fat: 8 g. – Sodium: 284 mg.
For exchange diets, count: 1 fruit, 1 fat, 1 lean meat.
Preparation time: 20 minutes. – Baking time: 15 minutes.

Used with permission of the innkeepers at The Log House & Homestead on Spirit Lake (see page 65)

SPINACH AND CRAB QUICHE
8 slices

9-inch refrigerated pie crust
1/2 of 10-ounce package Stauffer's
   frozen spinach soufflé
1/2 cup diced crabmeat (or 3 strips
   crisp bacon, crumbled)
1 cup shredded reduced-fat Swiss cheese

3 tablespoons grated Parmesan cheese
4 eggs or 1 cup liquid egg substitute
1 1/2 cups evaporated skim milk
1/8 teaspoon cayenne pepper
4 drops Tabasco sauce
paprika

1. Preheat oven to 375°.

2. Arrange pie crust in a 10-inch quiche dish.

3. Cut frozen spinach soufflé into cubes and place on top of crust. Sprinkle crab and cheeses over the top.

4. In a medium bowl, beat eggs, evaporated skim milk, pepper, and Tabasco sauce together. Pour over the crab, and sprinkle generously with paprika.

5. Bake for 40 minutes or until the center is set. Cool for 5 minutes before cutting into slices.

Calories per serving: 243 – Fat: 12 g. (Reduce fat to 5 g. by baking in a quiche pan without the pastry crust.) – Sodium: 398 mg. For exchange diets, count: 1 starch, 2 lean meat, 1 fat. Preparation time: 20 minutes. – Baking time: 40 minutes. Cooling time: 5 minutes.

Used with permission of the innkeepers at Abigail's "Elegant Victorian Mansion" (see page 12)

Country Victorian B & B

Mark & Becky Potter, Innkeepers
435 South Main Street
Middlebury, Indiana 46540
(219) 825-2568;
Toll free: (888) BNB-STAY (262-7829);
Fax: (219) 825-3411
e-mail: mark@michianatoday.com

Return to yesteryear in Northern Indiana's Amish country. Sit on the front porch and catch a passing buggy or relax on the back patio surrounded by an old-fashioned garden. Frozen Fruit Slush (page 2) has a nice berry color and tangy flavor, pleasing guests over and over. It is served as a complement to our breakfast entrées or as a refreshing snack or light dessert on a hot summer day.

STITT HOUSE BREAKFAST QUICHE
8 servings

6 eggs or 1 1/2 cups liquid
   egg substitute
2 cups skim milk
1 tablespoon chopped fresh chives
   (or 1/2 tablespoon dried)
1 tablespoon fresh chopped parsley
1/4 teaspoon salt
1/4 teaspoon ground pepper
2 cups grated reduced-fat cheese
   (mozzarella, Swiss, or cheddar)

1 cup cubed, sautéed, and drained
   bacon or ham (or your favorite
   combination of cooked lean meat
   and raw vegetables)
1/2 cup finely chopped onions,
   sautéed
5 English muffin halves, cut into
   very small cubes
Garnish: fresh parsley and salsa

1. Spray 8 ramekins thoroughly with nonstick cooking spray and pre-heat oven to 400°.

2. Beat first six ingredients together in a mixing bowl. Fold in cheese, bacon or ham, onions, and English muffins.

3. Ladle into ramekins and bake approximately 20 minutes. Serve in ramekin or loosen quiche with knife around edges and turn onto plate. Garnish with fresh parsley and serve with salsa.

Calories per serving: 206 – Fat: 8 g. – Sodium: 458 mg.
For exchange diets, count: 3 lean meat, 1/2 starch.
Preparation time: 15 minutes. – Baking time: 20 minutes.

Used with permission of the innkeepers at Stitt House Bed & Breakfast Inn (see page 37)

The Combes Family Inn

Ruth & Bill Combes, Innkeepers
RFD #1 Box 275
Ludlow, Vermont 05149
(802) 228-8799;
Toll free: (800) 822-8799
E-mail: billcfi@aol.com
www.combesfamilyinn.com

"Bring your family home to ours," say the proprietors of the Combes Family Inn. The inn, a local dairy farm for over a century, offers a quiet respite from the hustle of today's hectic life-style. The restored farmhouse is located on a quiet country road in the heart of Vermont's mountains and lakes region, with 50 acres of rolling meadows and woods to explore and to cross-country ski in winter. The inn has 11 cozy, country-inspired guest rooms, all with private baths. Pets are permitted in the units attached to the main house. Relax and socialize (BYOB) in the inn's "keeping room," furnished with turn-of-the-century oak. Sample Bill's country breakfasts and Ruth's delicious home cooking.

SUMMER VEGGIE PIE
1 10-inch pie, or 12 slices

nonstick cooking spray
1 pound frozen shredded potatoes, thawed
1 teaspoon Mrs. Dash seasoning
1 large onion, thinly sliced
4 green onions, chopped
1 teaspoon minced garlic
1 teaspoon vegetable oil
1 small stalk broccoli, chopped

1 small zucchini, sliced
1 cup thinly sliced mushrooms
1 pound extra firm tofu, drained
1 tablespoon vegetable oil
2 tablespoons lemon juice
1 teaspoon garlic powder or granules
1 teaspoon salt
3 tablespoons flour
paprika

1. Preheat oven to 350°.

2. Spray a 10-inch glass pie plate with cooking spray and place potatoes in the pan. Sprinkle with Mrs. Dash. Bake for 20 to 25 minutes, stirring occasionally, until slightly browned. As potatoes soften, spread evenly over bottom and side of pan.

3. In a skillet, sauté onions and garlic in oil until limp. Add broccoli, zucchini, and mushrooms, and sauté until tender. Transfer to a large mixing bowl. Set aside.

4. In a food processor or blender, blend tofu, oil, lemon juice, garlic powder, salt, and flour until very smooth. Add to vegetable mixture and stir.

5. Spread mixture evenly over potatoes in the pie pan. Sprinkle top with paprika. Bake for 45 minutes or until firm and lightly browned on top.

Calories per serving: 120 – Fat: 3 g. – Sodium: 189 mg.
For exchange diets, count: 1 starch, 1 vegetable, 1/2 fat.
Preparation time: 20 minutes. – Baking time: 70 minutes.

Used with permission of the innkeepers at Joshua Grindle Inn (see page 55)

ALMOST FAMOUS BREAKFAST PIZZA
3 pizzas, 6 servings each

5 cups bread flour
1 heaping tablespoon sugar
1 1/2 heaping tablespoons rapid-rise
  yeast
1/4 cup olive oil
1 3/4 cups hot water
cornmeal
1-2 teaspoons olive oil
Italian seasoned salt (recipe follows)
1/4 cup grated Romano cheese

8 ounces Italian sausage
2 cloves garlic
1/4 cup fresh parsley, minced
1 large onion, chopped
4 ounces reduced-fat cream cheese
1 1/2 cups nonfat ricotta cheese
1/2 cup grated Romano cheese
8 ounces mozzarella cheese, grated
3 medium tomatoes, chopped and
  drained

1. Stir flour, sugar, and yeast together in a large bowl. Combine olive oil and water; add all at once to dry ingredients, and mix until dough forms. Using a machine with dough hook or by hand, knead till smooth and elastic (3 to 5 minutes for machine and 10 minutes by hand).

2. Grease bowl with a little olive oil, turn dough to coat and cover with plastic wrap. Let rise in warm place until doubled, about 45 minutes. Punch down, re-cover, and let rise another 15 minutes.

3. For fantastic results, use a pizza stone, but you may use pans if you must! Place stone on lowest oven rack and preheat oven to 550° or the highest heat.

4. Divide dough into three equal parts and let stand for 5 minutes. Without rolling dough (which squishes out all the nice little bubbles), stretch, pull, or toss one part of dough till it is a 12-inch round. Place on pizza paddle or baking pan that has been well sprinkled with cornmeal.

5. Drizzle dough with a little olive oil (1 to 2 teaspoons) and brush to coat evenly. Sprinkle with Italian seasoned salt (see recipe that follows) and some grated Romano.

6. Slide dough onto stone or put pan in oven. Bake about 3 minutes or till dough has risen but is not browning. Remove from oven and repeat with other two pieces of dough.

7. Remove sausage from casing and crumble into medium frying pan. Sauté over medium heat. Mince garlic and parsley in food processor and add to the pan. Add onions to pan. Sauté until meat is no longer pink. Remove from heat and let cool.

8. Whip cream cheese and ricotta cheese in food processor, mixer, or by hand. Add the grated Romano and the cooled sausage mixture.

Divide mixture evenly over the three partially baked crusts. Sprinkle the mozzarella evenly over the pizzas. Top with chopped tomatoes.

9. Bake individually at 550° for 8 to 10 minutes or until cheese is bubbling and browning. Eat hot or at room temperature at any time of the day or night. These pizzas freeze well. Just wrap in plastic and foil.

Calories per serving: 275 – Fat: 10 g. – Sodium: 304 mg.
For exchange diets, count: 2 starch, 2 lean meat, 1 vegetable.
Preparation time: 25 minutes. Rising time: 1 hour. – Baking time: 15 minutes.

Used with permission of the innkeepers at The Little Blue House B&B (see next page)

TOASTED ALMOND AND ZUCCHINI QUICHE
6 servings

nonstick cooking spray	2 tablespoons sherry
1/4 cup grated Parmesan cheese	3 egg yolks
2 small zucchinis, sliced	1 cup skim milk
4 ounces fresh mushrooms, sliced	1/2 cup nonfat sour cream
2 green onions, chopped	1/2 teaspoon salt
2 Roma tomatoes, diced	1/2 teaspoon dry mustard
2 cloves garlic, minced	3 egg whites, beaten stiff
1 tablespoon butter-flavored margarine	2 tablespoons toasted almonds

1. Preheat oven to 350°.

2. Spray a 1 1/2-quart quiche dish with cooking spray.

3. Sprinkle cheese over the bottom of the dish. Sauté next six ingredients in a skillet over medium heat until vegetables are limp. Arrange vegetable mixture on top of the cheese.

4. Combine sherry, egg yolks, skim milk, sour cream, salt, and dry mustard with a whisk.

5. Beat egg whites until stiff; fold into yolk mixture. Gently pour over vegetables.

6. Sprinkle toasted almonds over top. Bake for 40 minutes or until center is set.

This recipe makes a crustless quiche. A second option is to bake the quiche in a potato crust (see recipe for Summer Veggie Pie [page 121] for potato crust). A third option is to bake the quiche in a pre-baked 10-inch pastry shell.

Calories per serving: 153 – Fat: 8 g. – Sodium: 344 mg.
For exchange diets, count: 1 lean meat, 2 vegetable, 1 fat.
Preparation time: 15 minutes. – Baking time: 40 minutes.

Used with permission of the innkeepers at Joshua Grindle Inn (see page 55)

The Little Blue House B & B

Michael & Margot Kornfeld, Innkeepers
115 Center Street
Lewiston, New York 14092
(716) 754-9425;
Toll free: (800) 636-0110;
Fax: (716) 754-8449
E-mail: mikek@wzrd.com

The Little Blue House B & B is located within what has been called "the most historic square mile in America." Situated in the village of Lewiston near the Niagara River, you can almost hear the powerful crashing of the famous Niagara Falls. The Little Blue House, a colonial, was built in 1906. Original paneling, French doors, and pine floors blend with a collection of antiques and contemporary art to create a warm, cozy ambiance. Breakfast is a social affair where guests meet to savor the deliciously different home baking, seasonal treats, and lively conversation.

ITALIAN SEASONED SALT
48 teaspoons

1/2 cup salt
1/4 cup garlic powder

1/4 cup oregano
2 teaspoons cayenne pepper

1. Blend all ingredients together thoroughly. Use this blend with breakfast pizza or to add a salty Italian flavor to plain foods.

Sodium per teaspoon: 1100 mg. – Negligible calories or fat.
Preparation time: 5 minutes.

Used with permission of the innkeepers at The Little Blue House B & B

BREAKFAST IN BREAD
8 servings

1 round sourdough loaf
8 ounces lean ham, cubed
1/3 bell pepper (green, red, or yellow), thinly sliced crosswise and sautéed briefly
3 ounces reduced-fat cheddar cheese, shredded or sliced

3 ounces reduced-fat Monterey Jack cheese, shredded or sliced
6 eggs, wet scrambled
2.5-ounce can ripe olives
1 medium tomato, thinly sliced
4-ounce can mushrooms or 8 ounces fresh mushrooms (sliced and cooked)

1. Preheat oven to 350°.

2. Cut the top off the loaf of bread; remove any bread from the cut-off crust with a spoon; set aside for lid. Remove soft interior of the loaf

with a spoon. Try to remove as much of the interior as possible without breaking through the crust. (Save the soft interior bread...it makes excellent bread crumbs.)

3. Place the ham in the bottom of the loaf. Top with bell peppers. Add a layer of half of the cheddar and Monterey Jack cheese. Then add the hot, slightly wet scrambled eggs. Use the back of a spoon to push the scrambled eggs into all sections of the loaf.

4. Add the olives. Spread the tomato slices on the olives. Add the rest of the cheeses. Top with mushrooms. Put on the lid. Double wrap the loaf tightly in heavy foil.

5. Bake for about 45 minutes. Remove from oven. Set aside for about 5 minutes to cool slightly. This keeps the cheese from running when you cut the loaf.

6. Cut the loaf into eight wedges with an electric knife. Place the Breakfast in Bread on a plate. Garnish with three or four leaves from a scented geranium. Place one or more edible flowers on the top and serve with a flair.

Calories per serving: 277 – Fat: 5 g. – Sodium: 577 mg.
For exchange diets, count: 2 starch, 1 vegetable, 2 lean meat.
Preparation time: 20 minutes. – Baking time: 45 minutes. Cooling time: 5 minutes.

Used with permission of the innkeeper at Mountain Laurel Inn

Mountain Laurel Inn

Sarah Wilcox, Innkeeper
624 Road 948
P.O. Box 443
Mentone, Alabama 35984
(205) 634-4673;
Toll free: (800) 889-4244

Mountain Laurel Inn is located in the woods on top of Lookout Mountain along the Little River near the historic town of Mentone. Mountain Laurel Inn is a guest house located in the woods about 200 feet from the hosts. Breakfast is served family-style in Sarah's home with a variety of selections. Upon arriving at the table, specialties such as zucchini, carrot, or lemon bread are always found. Each meal includes a hot fruit casserole or fresh fruit. The main offering may be such delights as Breakfast Pizza, Bagel Sandwiches, Egg & Sausage Casserole, Stuffed French Toast, Grits Casserole, or Eggs Rancheros, but Breakfast in Bread is the specialty.

BAKED EGGS IN CHEESY WILD RICE
8 servings

4 cups cooked wild rice (about 1 cup uncooked)

SAUCE:
1 tablespoon margarine
1 cup sliced fresh mushrooms
1 small green pepper, diced
1 small onion, minced

3 tablespoons flour
1 teaspoon salt
1/4 teaspoon white pepper
2 cups evaporated skim milk
4 ounces shredded reduced-fat Swiss cheese
8 eggs or 2 cups liquid egg substitute

1. Cook wild rice according to package directions.

2. Meanwhile, melt margarine in skillet. Sauté mushrooms, green pepper, and onion for 3 to 4 minutes.

3. Sprinkle in flour, salt, and pepper. Cook and stir until well blended. Slowly stir in evaporated skim milk, stirring constantly, until mixture begins to thicken. Add cheese and stir constantly until cheese melts. Remove from heat.

4. Preheat the oven to 350°.

5. Stir half of the cheese sauce into the cooked rice. Spread rice mixture in a shallow 7 x 11-inch casserole dish that has been heavily sprayed with nonstick cooking spray. (Select a dish that resists scorching.)

6. Make eight indentations in rice. Spread a spoonful of the remaining cheese in each indentation. Break 1 egg into each indentation.

7. Bake, uncovered, for 20 to 25 minutes, or until eggs are cooked as desired.

Calories per serving: 215 – Fat: 6 g. – Sodium: 492 mg.
For exchange diets, count: 1 starch, 1 vegetable, 1 lean meat, 1/2 skim milk.
Preparation time: 30 minutes. – Rice cooking time: 45 minutes.
Baking time: 25 minutes.

Used with permission of the innkeepers at Finnish Heritage Homestead Bed & Breakfast

Finnish Heritage Homestead
Bed & Breakfast

Elaine & Buzz Schultz, Innkeepers
4776 Waisanen Road
Embarrass, Minnesota 55732
(218) 984-3318;
Toll free: (800) 863-6545

Experience country tranquillity and hospitality that will be memorable. This 1901 historic Finnish American log farmstead provides an intimate atmosphere of antiques, heirlooms, and handmade rugs and quilts. Each morning you will awake to the crowing of the rooster and a full farm-family-style breakfast that features North Woods traditions. Buzz Schultz says Baked Eggs in Cheese Wild Rice is a favorite of B & B guests.

EGGS DERELICT
8 servings

2 cups skim milk, divided	8 eggs
2 tablespoons cornstarch	4 sliced English muffins
3 tablespoons sherry	2 teaspoons margarine
minced garlic to taste	1/2 cup grated Parmesan cheese
onion powder to taste	8 slices smoked turkey breast
salt to taste	chopped fresh dill
1/2 cup grated reduced-fat cheddar cheese	

1. Dissolve cornstarch in 1/4 cup of milk. Pour remaining milk into a saucepan, then whisk in the cornstarch slurry. Cook over medium heat until thick. Add sherry and spices; stir until blended. Add cheese and stir until melted. Keep sauce warm.

2. Meanwhile, poach eggs.

3. Spread English muffins with margarine and sprinkle with Parmesan cheese. Heat large skillet and toast English muffins buttered side down until toasted.

4. On a plate, layer toast (cheese side up), turkey, and poached eggs. Pour sherry cheese sauce over egg stack, sprinkle with chopped dill, and serve immediately.

Calories per serving: 194 – Fat: 4 g. – Sodium: 316 mg.
For exchange diets, count: 1 starch, 2 lean meat.
Preparation time: 20 minutes.

Used with permission of the innkeepers at Old Town B & B Inn (see page 97)

EGG TRUFFLES WITH CANADIAN BACON
4 servings

4 slices white or nut-grain bread
1 cup shredded reduced-fat mild
   cheddar cheese
2 green onions, chopped
4 slices grilled Canadian bacon,
   finely chopped

1/2 teaspoon garlic powder
1/2 teaspoon basil
4 eggs or 1 cup liquid egg substitute
1/2 teaspoon paprika

1. Preheat oven to 350°.

2. Mold bread slices to fit into a well-greased Texas muffin pan. Sprinkle shredded cheese, green onions, and chopped Canadian bacon into each bread basket. Add a pinch of garlic powder and a pinch of basil to each basket.

3. Beat eggs and pour over mixture in each basket, covering ingredients.

4. Bake for 20 minutes or until eggs puff up.

5. Gently lift egg truffles out of pan onto serving dish. Top with paprika and serve.

Optional: Heat a prepared hollandaise sauce and serve over truffles.

Calories per serving: 241 – Fat: 9 g. – Sodium: 752 mg.
For exchange diets, count: 1 starch, 3 lean meat.
Preparation time: 15 minutes. – Baking time: 20 minutes.

Used with permission of the innkeepers at Country Suite "A Noteworthy B & B"

Country Suite "A Noteworthy B & B"

Lorraine Seidel & Sondra Clark, Innkeepers
Route 23, P.O. Box 700
Windham, New York 12496
(518) 734-4079;
Toll free: (800) LAND-SKY;
Fax: (518) 734-4079
E-mail: ctrysuite@aol.com

Nestled deep in the heart of Greene County's Catskill Mountains, this retreat features a fabulous gourmet breakfast of splendid dishes, such as pear-filled French vanilla toast or eggs Benedict.

Mountain Creek Bed & Breakfast

Hylah & Guy Smalley, Innkeepers
100 Chestnut Walk Drive
Waynesville, North Carolina 28786
(704) 456-5509;
Toll free: (800) 557-9766
E-mail: Guylah@aol.com
www.sogospel.com/mcbb

In 1995, Hylah and Guy took a cycling ride on their tandem bicycle through the Smokies looking for property to develop into a bed and breakfast and fell in love with this diamond in the rough. The inn is located in Waynesville, a quaint town full of antique shops, four-star restaurants, and a folk festival. Guests dine in or out on the 1600-square-foot deck that wraps around the west side of the house overlooking the creek, trout pond, and mountain. There is also a cool and refreshing lap pool with a private deck for those wishing to sun. Hylah is a self-described "health nut" and helped Guy lose 50 pounds while they were dating!

EGG TRUFFLES
6 servings

nonstick cooking spray
6 slices honey wheat bread
1/2 cup fresh mushrooms, sliced
2 ounces reduced-fat cheddar cheese, grated

2 green onions
1/2 teaspoon garlic powder
6 eggs
1 can cream of potato soup, warmed through

1. Preheat oven to 350°.

2. Spray a Texas muffin tin with cooking spray.

3. Put one slice of bread in each muffin cup, so the bread forms a basket.

4. Add a sprinkle of mushrooms, cheese, and green onions.

5. Add a dash of garlic powder.

6. Crack one egg into each basket.

7. Bake for 10 to 15 minutes. Do not overbake. The egg should be all white.

8. Add a few spoonfuls of soup over each truffle.

Calories per serving: 207 – Fat: 9 g. – Sodium: 413 mg.
For exchange diets, count: 1 lean meat, 1 fat, 1 starch, 1 vegetable.
Preparation time: 15 minutes. – Baking time: 15 minutes.

Used with permission of the innkeepers at Mountain Creek Bed & Breakfast

River House Bed & Breakfast

Kate & Lars Enggren and Crystal Carroll,
Innkeepers
495 Animas View Drive
Durango, Colorado 81301
(970) 247-4775;
Toll free: (800) 254-4775;
Fax: (970) 259-1465

The River House is a seven bedroom, southwestern style home located on the north edge of Durango facing the Animas River. With over 6500 square feet of living and common space, one never feels crowded. Deer and elk are often found feeding in our yard or seen grazing in the fields across the river. In the winter skiers can take full advantage of Durango's nightlife and in the morning be greeted by a ski area shuttle bus right at our front door. Upon your return a soothing soak in our therapeutic spa, perhaps followed by a revitalizing massage (two full-time trained massage therapists are on staff), or a hypnosis session will remind you why you chose Colorado and the River House as your ski destination.

EGGS FLORENTINE
8 squares

nonstick cooking spray
1 tablespoon margarine
1 sweet red onion, diced
10-ounce package frozen chopped
   spinach, thawed
2 tablespoons maple syrup
2 tablespoons pine (or piñon) nuts,
   chopped
8 eggs or 2 cups liquid egg substitute

1 tablespoon fresh basil
1/4 cup evaporated skim milk
1 ounce feta cheese (preferably
   flavored with basil and sun-dried
   tomatoes)
Optional sauce: hollandaise prepared
   from dry mix
Optional garnish: 1 tablespoon finely
   grated lemon rind

1. Preheat oven to 350°.

2. Spray a 9 x 13-inch pan with cooking spray.

2. Melt margarine in a skillet; sauté onion in the margarine for 3 minutes. Add chopped spinach and sauté 5 more minutes.

3. Stir in maple syrup and pine nuts. Spread this mixture in the prepared 9 x 13-inch pan. Set aside.

5. Beat eggs. Add basil and evaporated skim milk.

6. Scramble in a skillet. As eggs start to cook, add feta cheese with basil and sun-dried tomatoes. Finish scrambling eggs and pour over the spinach mixture.

7. If you use a hollandaise sauce, spoon it over the eggs before baking.

8. Garnish with finely grated lemon rind. Bake for 15 minutes.

Calories per serving: 117 – Fat: 6 g. – Sodium: 216 mg.
For exchange diets, count: 1 1/2 lean meat, 1 vegetable.
Preparation time: 15 minutes. – Baking time: 15 minutes.

Used with permission of the innkeepers at River House Bed & Breakfast

FESTIVE EGG SQUARES
12 servings

nonstick cooking spray
1/2 pound reduced-fat sausage,
  cooked and drained
4 ounces fresh mushrooms, sliced
2 green onions, chopped
2 medium tomatoes, chopped
2 cups shredded part-skim mozzarella
  cheese

12 eggs or 3 cups liquid egg substitute
1 cup skim milk
1/2 teaspoon salt
1/2 teaspoon pepper
1/2 teaspoon oregano
1 1/4 cups reduced-fat baking mix

1. Preheat oven to 350°.

2. Generously spray a 9 x 13-inch baking pan with cooking spray.

3. Layer cooked sausage, mushrooms, green onions, tomatoes, and cheese in baking dish.

4. In a mixing bowl, beat together remaining ingredients and pour over sausage and vegetables.

5. Bake for 30 minutes or until golden brown. This dish may be prepared the night before, covered, and baked the next morning.

Serving suggestion: Pass the picante sauce to top the egg dish.

Calories per serving: 204 – Fat: 7 g. – Sodium: 483 mg.
For exchange diets, count: 2 lean meat, 1 starch, 1 vegetable.
Preparation time: 15 minutes. – Baking time: 30 minutes.

Used with permission of the innkeeper at Hideaway Inn Bed & Breakfast

Hideaway Inn Bed & Breakfast

Julia Baldridge, Innkeeper
Rt. 1 Box 199, County Road #82
Hardy, Arkansas 72542
(501) 966-4770

This secluded country home and log cabin offer
376 acres of privacy, with a variety of wildlife and
birds, a private fishing hole, picnic sites, and swimming hole.

HOPPEL POPPEL

8 servings

4 large Idaho baking potatoes
1 tablespoon vegetable oil
1 medium sweet onion, chopped
8 ounces lean cooked chicken, pork, or roast beef, chopped
1 tablespoon chopped fresh parsley
1 tablespoon chopped fresh chives
1/4 teaspoon salt
1/4 teaspoon pepper
1/4 teaspoon minced garlic
8 eggs, beaten, or 2 cups liquid egg substitute
1/4 cup milk

1. Cut potatoes into slices with the skins on. Sprinkle with 2 tablespoons of water, cover, and microwave for 8 minutes.

2. Heat oil in a large skillet; add meat and onions, and cook over medium heat for 10 minutes, stirring occasionally.

3. In a separate bowl, beat parsley, chives, salt, pepper, garlic, egg or egg substitute, and milk; stir in cooked meat.

4. Add the potatoes to the egg and meat mixture.

5. Cook over medium heat for 10 minutes or until eggs are fluffy. Serve hot.

Calories per serving: 213 – Fat: 4 g. – Sodium: 201 mg.
For exchange diets, count: 2 lean meat, 1 1/2 starch.
Preparation time: 25 minutes.

Used with permission of the innkeepers at Flemingsburg House Bed & Breakfast at Sweetwater Farm (see page 6)

Chestnut Charm Bed and Breakfast

Barbara Stensvad, Innkeeper
1409 Chestnut Street
Atlantic, Iowa 50022
(712) 243-5652

This enchanting country inn is an 1898 Victorian mansion with sunrooms, fireplaces, original hand-painted linen wallcoverings by a depression-era artist, patio with large fountain, and 12-foot gazebo. The elegant guest rooms have private baths. Awaken to the aromas of gourmet coffee and home-baking. Other exquisite gourmet meals are available with advance reservations. The handicap-accessible renovated carriage house has four suites, including whirlpool tubs for two, in-room fireplaces, a sauna, and many other amenities. It's a short drive to the famous bridges of Madison County.

FLORENTINE BENEDICT
4 servings

2 large potatoes
nonstick cooking spray
4 eggs, poached
4 slices bacon, cooked, drained,
    and crumbled
1 tablespoon margarine
2 tablespoons flour
1 1/4 cups skim milk
1/8 teaspoon white pepper

1/4 teaspoon dry mustard
1 tablespoon chopped chives
1/2 cup (2 ounces) shredded
    reduced-fat cheddar cheese
1 pound fresh spinach leaves,
    washed and torn into small pieces
1/4 pound mushrooms, cleaned,
    trimmed, and sliced
4 thin red onion slices

1. Wash and pierce potatoes with a fork. Cut potatoes in half and cook unpeeled potatoes in the microwave on high power for 5 to 7 minutes. Set aside to cool slightly. When cool enough to touch, dice into 1/2-inch cubes and brown over medium-low heat in skillet sprayed with cooking spray.

2. While potatoes are cooking, poach eggs and cook bacon.

3. Melt margarine in a heavy saucepan over medium heat.

4. In a shaker container, combine flour, milk, pepper, mustard, and chives. Shake vigorously until well mixed. Pour into margarine and cook over medium heat until bubbly and thick. Stir in cheese.

5. To assemble this egg entrée: Divide diced potatoes into four portions. Place on warmed dinner plates. Place spinach on top of hot potatoes. Sprinkle with bacon, mushrooms, and onion slices. Place a poached egg on each plate. Pour sauce over all and serve immediately.

Calories per serving: 303 – Fat: 11 – Sodium: 359 mg.
For exchange diets, count: 1 1/2 starch, 1 vegetable, 2 lean meat, 1 fat.
Preparation time: 25 minutes.

Used with permission of the innkeeper at Chestnut Charm Bed and Breakfast

Hash Brown and Sausage Mini-Frittatas

6 servings, 2 mini-frittatas each

nonstick cooking spray
1/4 cup spicy turkey sausage
1 small onion, chopped fine
1 1/2 cups frozen hash brown potatoes, thawed
1/2 teaspoon minced garlic
1 teaspoon dried oregano
1 teaspoon dried thyme
1/2 teaspoon salt

1/2 teaspoon pepper
1/3 cup water
3 large eggs or 3/4 cup liquid egg substitute
2 large egg whites, beaten
1 cup nonfat buttermilk
1/4 cup grated Parmesan cheese
2 tablespoons flour
1 cup prepared salsa

1. Preheat oven to 350°.

2. Spray 12 muffin cups with cooking spray.

3. In a medium skillet, cook sausage until browned. Remove sausage and drain.

4. Add onions and potatoes to skillet and cook until golden brown, about 10 minutes. Stir in garlic, oregano, thyme, salt, pepper, and drained sausage. Cook for 1 more minute.

5. Add water and cook just until water is evaporated.

6. In a medium bowl, whisk eggs, beaten egg whites, buttermilk, cheese, and flour. Add sausage and vegetable mixture.

7. Spoon mixture into prepared muffin cups and bake for 20 minutes or just until frittatas are golden on top.

8. Use a knife to loosen them from pan and serve with salsa.

Calories per serving: 157 – Fat: 7 g. – Sodium: 371 mg.
For exchange diets, count: 1 starch, 1 vegetable, 1 lean meat.
Preparation time: 20 minutes. – Baking time: 20 minutes.

Used with permission of the innkeepers at Bauer Haus Bed & Breakfast (see page 34)

HAM AND EGG BAKE WITH CROUTONS
4 servings

nonstick cooking spray
1 cup stuffing mix or croutons
4 slices cooked ham or Canadian bacon
1 cup grated reduced-fat cheddar
  or Swiss cheese

4 large eggs or 1 cup liquid
  egg substitute
dash black pepper

1. Preheat oven to 325°.

2. Spray an 8-inch square pan with cooking spray.

3. Spread the stuffing mix in dish.

4. Place the ham or Canadian bacon on top of the stuffing mix and arrange half the grated cheese on top.

5. Carefully break eggs over the cheese, keeping the yolks whole. Season with pepper. Cover the eggs with remaining cheese and bake for 15 to 20 minutes or until yolks are firm.

Calories per serving: 183 – Fat: 7 g. – Sodium: 472 mg.
For exchange diets, count: 2 lean meat, 1 starch.
Preparation time: 15 minutes. – Baking time: 20 minutes.

Used with permission of the innkeepers at Cinnamon Hill Bed & Breakfast

Cinnamon Hill Bed & Breakfast

Shirley & Maurice DeVrient, Innkeepers
24 Wildwood Lane
Kimberling City, Missouri 65686
(417) 739-5727;
Toll free: (800) 925-1556

Shirley serves a full breakfast of juice, fresh fruit, and homemade pastries, cinnamon coffee cake, or muffins; as well as homemade jellies and jams. Her entrée menu varies, and might include a breakfast casserole, bacon or sausage, scrambled eggs, biscuits and gravy, or waffles and ham. Guests won't go away hungry.

HUEVOS RANCHEROS
8 servings

nonstick cooking spray
1 large Spanish onion, coarsely diced
4 cloves garlic, minced
1 green bell pepper, coarsely diced
1 red bell pepper, coarsely diced
1 tablespoon chili powder
1 teaspoon dried oregano
ground red pepper to taste
8-ounce can tomato paste

28-ounce can crushed tomatoes
1/2 cup red wine
8 small corn tortillas
2 cups shredded reduced-fat sharp
  cheddar cheese
16 eggs or 4 cups liquid egg
  substitute
grated Parmesan cheese
cayenne pepper to taste

1. Spray a deep iron skillet or a heavy Dutch oven with cooking spray and sauté the onions until they are soft and translucent. Add the garlic and continue to sauté over medium heat until both are lightly browned. Add both bell peppers and continue to cook until they are softened.

2. Add the seasonings and tomato paste, and combine thoroughly with the onion, garlic, and peppers, allowing the mixture to coat the bottom of the pan and brown. (Don't be concerned about a darker brown coloring as this is essential in bringing out the rich flavors of the combination of ingredients.)

3. Add the crushed tomatoes and the red wine and blend the mixture completely. Simmer uncovered for at least 30 minutes.

4. The mixture (or base) may be refrigerated overnight or it may be frozen for future use. (Hint: Since this is the most time consuming part of the preparation, make two or three times the amount called for in the recipe to divide up, freeze, and save for future use. If the base is cold, warm it before continuing.)

5. Preheat oven to 400°.

6. In eight individual oven-proof serving dishes, place one tortilla on the bottom and then cover with the base to a depth of about 1/2 inch. Cover the warm base with a generous layer of cheddar cheese. Break two eggs or 1/2 cup liquid egg substitute over the eggs and cheese, keeping the yolks whole. Sprinkle a covering layer of Parmesan cheese over the eggs, and shake a bit of cayenne pepper over the top.

7. Bake for 25 minutes or until the eggs are firm, and serve with jalapeño corn bread.

Calories per serving: 266 – Fat: 9 g. – Sodium: 682 mg.
For exchange diets, count: 1 starch, 2 lean meat, 1/2 skim milk, 1 vegetable.
Preparation time: 45 minutes. – Baking time: 25 minutes.

Used with permission of the innkeepers at Birchwood Inn (see page 144)

NEWFOUNDLAND FRITTATA
4 servings

1 tablespoon olive oil
1/4 teaspoon crushed garlic
1/2 cup cooked vegetables
1/4 cup sliced fresh mushrooms
1 green onion, finely chopped
1/2 green or red pepper, finely chopped
1/4 to 1/2 cup cooked fish (such as cod
   or salmon), diced

6 eggs or 1 1/2 cups liquid egg
   substitute
1/4 cup skim milk
1/4 teaspoon salt
1/8 teaspoon cayenne or black pepper

1. Preheat oven to 325°.

2. Heat the oil and garlic in a heavy oven-proof skillet at medium heat and sauté vegetables, mushrooms, onions, and peppers for 2 minutes. Reduce heat to low and add fish.

3. Meanwhile, combine eggs or egg substitute, milk, salt, and pepper, beat for 30 seconds, and stir into heated mixture. Allow mixture to warm through again, about 2 minutes, stir gently, and place in oven for 4 or 5 minutes. Serve at once.

Calories per serving: 151 – Fat: 5 g. – Sodium: 384 mg.
For exchange diets, count: 2 lean meat, 1 vegetable.
Preparation time: 15 minutes. – Baking time: 5 minutes.

Used with permission of the innkeeper at The Gower House

The Gower House

Len Clark, Innkeeper
180 Gower Street
St. John's, Newfoundland
A1C 2A5
(709) 754-0047

Gower House is a refurbished heritage town-
house designated by the Newfoundland Historic Trust. This dish was created at a post-skiing party when a local girl whipped up a delicious breakfast using leftovers from the previous evening's meal.

ONE-SERVING CHEESE PUFF
1 serving

1 slice bread
1/2 teaspoon margarine
1/4 cup grated reduced-fat cheese
1 egg or 1/4 cup liquid egg substitute

1/2 cup skim milk
dash onion salt
dash hot sauce

1. Preheat oven to 350°.

2. Spread margarine on bread and place buttered side down in a large greased custard cup.

3. In a small bowl, mix rest of ingredients and pour over bread. Place custard cup on baking sheet and bake for 35 to 40 minutes.

This recipe is easy to double, triple, or whatever. Chopped ham or crumbled bacon makes a nice addition.

> Calories per serving: 207 – Fat: 5 g. – Sodium: 471 mg.
> For exchange diets, count: 1 starch, 1/2 skim milk, 1 1/2 lean meat.
> Preparation time: 10 minutes – Baking time: 40 minutes.

Used with permission of the innkeeper at Rocking Horse Manor Bed & Breakfast (see page 35)

OVERNIGHT GRITS & SAUSAGE CASSEROLE
12 squares

1/2 pound mild reduced-fat pork
  sausage (suggest Jones Dairy
  Farm variety)
3/4 cup uncooked quick-cooking grits
  (not instant)
6 eggs, beaten, or 1 1/2 cups liquid
  egg substitute

1 cup skim milk
1/4 teaspoon garlic salt
1/4 teaspoon pepper
1 slice white bread, crusts removed,
  torn into 1-inch pieces
4 ounces shredded reduced-fat
  extra sharp cheddar cheese

1. Cook sausage over medium heat until browned, stirring to crumble. Drain well and set aside.

2. Cook grits according to package directions. Set aside.

3. In large bowl, beat eggs or egg substitute. Add milk, garlic salt, and pepper; beat again. Stir in bread pieces. Stir in shredded cheese and cooked grits until cheese starts to melt. Stir in cooked, drained sausage. Refrigerate overnight.

4. In the morning spread mixture in lightly greased 9 x 13-inch baking dish and bake in preheated 350° oven, uncovered, 1 hour or until set. Let cooked casserole cool for 10 to 15 minutes before serving.

> Calories per serving: 132 – Fat: 5 g. – Sodium: 321 mg.
> For exchange diets, count: 1 1/2 lean meat, 1/2 starch.
> Preparation time: 20 minutes. Refrigeration time: overnight. – Baking time: 1 hour.

Used with permission of the innkeepers at Bay Avenue's Sunset Bed & Breakfast (see page 75)

HUEVOS ROJOS ENCHILADAS
10 servings

nonstick cooking spray
1/2 cup chopped red bell pepper
8-ounce package reduced-fat
  cream cheese
1/2 cup salsa
1/2 cup chopped onion

10 eggs, scrambled and seasoned
10 flour tortillas
1 1/2 cups shredded reduced-fat
  Monterey Jack cheese
Garnish: chopped green onion
  and tomatoes

1. Preheat oven to 350°. Spray two 11 x 7-inch baking dishes with cooking spray.

2. Place pepper, cream cheese, salsa, and onion in a blender and process until smooth.

3. Gently combine 3/4 cup of this mixture with the scrambled eggs.

4. Spoon 1/3 cup of the egg mixture down the center of each tortilla, roll up, and place seam side down in the baking dishes. Spoon remaining sauce over the enchiladas. Cover with foil and refrigerate overnight or bake.

5. Bake for 25 minutes. Sprinkle with cheese and bake 5 more minutes. Garnish with chopped green onions and fresh tomatoes.

Calories per serving: 263 – Fat: 11 g. – Sodium: 694 mg.
(To reduce sodium, use less salsa.)
For exchange diets, count: 2 starch, 2 lean meat.
Preparation time: 20 minutes. – Baking time: 30 minutes.

Used with permission of the innkeeper at Abriendo Inn (see page 7)

ROSIE'S EGGS MEXICANA

6 servings

nonstick cooking spray
1 1/4 cups liquid egg substitute
1/4 cup all-purpose flour
1/4 teaspoon baking powder
2 tablespoons liquid Butter Buds

1 cup nonfat cottage cheese
1 1/2 cups shredded reduced-fat
   Monterey Jack cheese
4-ounce can chopped green chiles

1. Preheat oven to 350°.

2. Spray a quiche dish or large pie plate with cooking spray.

3. Mix egg substitute, flour, baking powder, and Butter Buds together in a mixing bowl. Add the cheeses and chiles; stir to mix.

4. Pour into prepared pan and bake for 30 minutes or until slightly browned on top and puffed up. Let stand 5 minutes before serving. Serve with salsa and/or nonfat sour cream.

Calories per serving: 138 – Fat: 5 g. – Sodium: 333 mg.
For exchange diets, count: 2 lean meat, 1 vegetable.
Preparation time: 15 minutes. – Baking time: 30 minutes.
Standing time: 5 minutes.

Used with permission of the innkeeper at Bauer Haus Bed & Breakfast (see page 34)

St. Augustine's Cedar House Inn
Victorian B and B

Nina & Russ Thomas, Innkeepers
79 Cedar Street
St. Augustine, Florida 32084
(904) 829-0079;
Toll free: (800) 233-2746;
Fax: (904) 825-0916
E-mail: russ@aug.com
http://www.cedarhouseinn.com

Relax and enjoy historic St. Augustine, Florida, at the restored 1893 home of innkeepers Russ and Nina Thomas. At this beautiful Victorian inn, located within an easy walk to shops, restaurants, and historic sites, the emphasis is on hospitality and comfortable surroundings in a personal atmosphere. The full gourmet breakfast is a special occasion. Nina takes pride in setting an elegant table with lace, fine china, and gold ware. Each morning's table setting is a surprise chosen from over 12 different table settings and china ware. Russ's culinary expertise and imaginative menus are gaining widespread appreciation and acclaim. Special dinners and picnics are available with prior arrangements.

RUSS'S RUFFLED EGGS
6 servings

nonstick cooking spray
6 slices honey wheat bread
6 eggs or 1 1/2 cups liquid
   egg substitute
dash of garlic powder
salt
pepper
1/2 cup grated Parmesan cheese

1/2 of 14.5-ounce can yams, drained
   and diced
10-ounce can reduced-fat cream of
   chicken soup
5 ounces skim milk (1/2 soup can)
2 small tomatoes, sliced
1 green onion, chopped

1. Preheat oven to 350°.

2. Spray a 6-compartment Texas muffin tin with cooking spray, and press in slices of bread to make bread shells.

3. Break an egg into each of the bread shells.

4. Sprinkle a dash of garlic powder on top of each egg plus a dash each of salt and pepper. Top with a little cheese.

5. Bake for approximately 20 minutes, or until egg sets.

6. Combine yams with soup and milk. Heat for 3 minutes on high in the microwave.

7. Top each egg with yam sauce, tomato slices, and chopped green onions.

Calories per serving: 227 mg. – Fat: 6 g. – Sodium: 560 mg.
For exchange diets, count: 2 starch, 1 lean meat.
Preparation time: 15 minutes. – Baking time: 20 minutes.

Used with permission of the innkeepers at St. Augustine's Cedar House Inn Victorian B and B

SAFFRON CREAM EGGS

12 servings

2 cups evaporated skim milk
1 tablespoon margarine
1/2 cup shredded sharp cheddar cheese
1/8 teaspoon saffron
1/2 teaspoon Lawry seasoning salt
1/2 teaspoon white pepper

1/4 cup pecans
1/2 teaspoon cayenne pepper
1/2 teaspoon paprika
1/2 teaspoon cinnamon
12 eggs

1. Heat milk and margarine in a saucepan over medium heat. Add cheese and stir to melt. Add seasonings and pecans; blend. Place eggs gently into sauce, preserving yolks. Cook until desired doneness.

2. To serve, carefully place egg on plate and spoon sauce over the top.

Calories per serving: 160 – Fat: 10 g. – Sodium: 235 mg.
For exchange diets, count: 1 lean meat, 1/2 skim milk, 1 fat.
Preparation time: 15 minutes.

Used with permission of the innkeepers at Saltair Bed & Breakfast and Alpine Cottages (see page 2)

The Oliver Inn B & B

Richard & Venera Monahan, Innkeepers
630 West Washington Street
South Bend, Indiana 46601
(219) 232-4545;
Fax: (219) 288-9788
E-mail oliver@michiana.org

The Victorian romance of The Oliver Inn Bed and Breakfast reflects the lives and times of South Bend's most famous families, the Studebakers (wagons and automobiles) and the Olivers (Oliver plow and tractors). While Clem Studebaker was busy in August of 1896 building the foundation for his castle/home, Tippecanoe Place, James Oliver acquired the adjoining property. Here he built a spacious 10,000 square foot Queen Anne style home and gave it to his daughter, Josephine Oliver Ford, for "$1.00 and love." The hearty continental breakfast is in addition to the complimentary snacks and beverages in the butler's pantry 24 hours a day.

SPINACH & EGGS GREENBRIER
6 servings

nonstick cooking spray
2 packages frozen chopped spinach
4 slices bacon, diced
1/4 teaspoon minced garlic
1/2 teaspoon salt

1/4 teaspoon pepper
2 tablespoons grated Parmesan cheese
6 eggs, beaten well, or 1 1/2 cup
  liquid egg substitute

1. Preheat oven to 350°.

2. Spray a 1 1/2-quart baking dish with cooking spray.

3. Cook spinach and drain well.

4. Meanwhile, cook diced bacon until crisp; drain and remove from pan.

5. Sauté minced garlic in skillet; add spinach, salt, and pepper, and warm through.

6. Transfer spinach mixture to the prepared dish; sprinkle with Parmesan cheese, and pour beaten eggs over the spinach. Crumble bacon on top and bake for 30 minutes.

Calories per serving: 86 – Fat: 4 g. – Sodium: 310 mg.
For exchange diets, count: 2 vegetable, 1 fat.
Preparation time: 15 minutes. – Baking time: 30 minutes.

Used with permission of the innkeepers at Little Greenbrier Lodge Bed and Breakfast (see page 3)

TURKEY AND BROCCOLI OVERNIGHT EGG BAKE
16 squares

nonstick cooking spray
8 slices wheat bread, cubed
2 pounds turkey or turkey ham, cubed
2 10-ounce packages frozen chopped broccoli
2 4-ounce cans sliced mushrooms, drained
6 eggs or 1 1/2 cups liquid egg substitute

1 1/2 teaspoons garlic powder
1 1/2 teaspoons onion powder
3 cups skim milk
4 tablespoons flour
2 tablespoons prepared mustard
8 ounces fat-free mozzarella cheese

1. Preheat oven to 375° if baking immediately. Spray a 9 x 13-inch pan with cooking spray.

2. Layer bread, turkey, broccoli, and mushrooms in pan. Set aside.

3. In a mixing bowl, beat eggs, garlic powder, onion powder, milk, flour, and mustard until smooth. Pour into the pan; cover and refrigerate overnight if desired.

4. Cover and bake for 30 minutes. Sprinkle with cheese and bake uncovered 15 more minutes. Remove from oven and allow to set for 5 minutes before serving. Cut into 16 squares.

Calories per serving: 186 – Fat: 6 g. – Sodium: 766 mg.
For exchange diets, count: 1/2 starch, 1/2 skim milk, 1 lean meat,
1 vegetable, 1/2 fat. – Preparation time: 15 minutes. – Baking time: 45 minutes.
Resting time: 5 minutes.

Used with permission of the innkeepers at Parson's Inn Bed and Breakfast (see page 28)

Birchwood Inn

Joan, Dick, Anne & Dan Toner, Innkeepers
7 Hubbard Street
Lenox, Massachusetts 01240
(413) 637-2600; Toll free: (800) 524-1646
E-mail: detoner@bcn.net

Built in 1767, the Birchwood Inn is the only Lenox inn on the National Register of Historic Places. Lenox's first town meeting was held here in 1767. Today, Birchwood is known throughout the region for its warmth and hospitality. Breakfasts at the Birchwood are imaginative multi-course meals. While enjoying a buffet table of fruits, cereals, and muffins, the taste-tempting hot entree-of-the-day is being prepared. On weekend afternoons, wine and cheese are offered to the guests in the library or on the porch. Picnic hampers and blankets are available for guests who want to go to the park or the hills.

TARTE D'ALSACE
8 slices

2 large Spanish onions
1 tablespoon unsalted butter
2 tablespoons sugar
1 slight dash liquid smoke (optional)
3 eggs or 3/4 cup liquid egg substitute

1 cup nonfat sour cream
salt and pepper to taste
1 uncooked 9-inch pie crust
1/4 cup diced, broiled bacon bits, drained

1. Preheat oven to 400°.

2. Peel and slice the onions, across the rings, in slices about 1/2-inch wide, and then cut again at 90 degrees so you have pieces roughly 1/2-inch wide by 1 1/2-inches long.

3. Melt butter in a large, heavy iron skillet or in a heavy Dutch oven until bubbling. Add the onions and sauté on medium-high heat. When onions turn slightly brown, add the sugar and a dash of liquid smoke and then continue to brown the onions. Continue stirring the mixture, cooking until the onions are a rich chocolate-brown color. This may take up to 30 minutes, but is the key to the full flavor of the authentic tarte.

4. Set the onions aside to cool. Beat the eggs or liquid egg substitute and blend in the sour cream, salt, and pepper. When the pan that you used to cook the onions is cool enough to touch, add the egg and sour cream mixture. Whisk together well, picking up all the browned coating on the pan.

5. Pour the egg mixture into the uncooked pie shell. Sprinkle the bacon bits on top.

6. Bake for 1 hour or until the top of the pie is a rich golden brown and the crust is crisp. Serve immediately. Excellent as a main course for lunch or brunch or as a starter for formal dinners.

Hints

- Onions may be sautéed a day in advance and the final preparation begun just prior to baking.

- Pre-baked pie crusts are not recommended since the long cooking time for the quiche mixture might cause the exposed crust to burn.

- The liquid smoke provides a very authentic flavor to the tarte since the Alsatians normally bake this quiche in wood ovens.

Calories per serving: 209 – Fat: 11 g. – Sodium: 242 mg.
For exchange diets, count: 1 starch, 1/2 lean meat, 1 vegetable, 2 fat.
Preparation time: 40 minutes. – Baking time: 1 hour.

Used with permission of the innkeepers at Birchwood Inn

Potatoes and Side Dishes

CREAMY HASH BROWNS WITH CHICKEN, MUSHROOMS, AND CHEESE

24 1/2-cup servings

2 pounds frozen shredded
hash browns, thawed

1 can reduced-fat condensed
cream of mushroom soup

1 can reduced-fat condensed
cream of chicken soup

2 cups (8 ounces) grated reduced-fat
sharp cheddar cheese

1/2 cup reduced-fat ranch salad
dressing

2.8-ounce can fried onion rings

1. Mix together all ingredients except the onion rings in a 13 x 9-inch baking pan coated with nonstick cooking spray. Cover the pan and refrigerate overnight.

2. Next morning, remove the pan from the refrigerator and preheat the oven to 350°.

3. Bake uncovered for 55 minutes or until bubbly. Do not allow the edges to burn. Spread the onion rings over the top of the dish and return to the oven for 5 minutes.

Calories per serving: 133 – Fat: 3 g. – Sodium: 258 mg.
For exchange diets, count: 1 1/2 starch.
Preparation time: 10 minutes. – Refrigeration time: overnight. – Baking time: 60 minutes.

Used with permission of the innkeepers at The Ashwood (see page 98)

Inn at Poplar Corner

**Tom & Jacque Derrickson and
David & Jo Anne Snead, Innkeepers**
4248 Main Street
Chincoteague, Virginia 23336
(757) 336-6115;
Toll free: (800) 336-6787;
Fax: (757) 336-5776

Chincoteague's Inn at Poplar Corner was affectionately created and designed by David and Jo Anne Snead and Tom and Jacque Derrickson of the Watson House Bed and Breakfast. The Inn at Poplar Corner is a 2-1/2 story Victorian Home with five gables, three dormers, and a wrap-around verandah, all accented with gingerbread. Once in the door, feel at home and gaze through the parlor at the eclectic mix of antiques, wall coverings, fabrics, collectible treasures, and personal touches. The Inn at Poplar Corner provides a full gourmet breakfast every day.

FAT-FREE HOME FRIES
6 1-cup servings

6 small potatoes, washed, quartered,
and cut into wedges
1/4 cup water or chicken broth
nonstick cooking spray

Cajun seasoning to taste
(suggest 1/2 teaspoon)
salt to taste (suggest 1/2 teaspoon)

1. Preheat oven to 350°.

2. Place prepared potatoes in a microwave-safe baking dish. Sprinkle with water or chicken broth and cover. Microwave on high power for 6 to 8 minutes or until potatoes are tender when pierced with a fork.

3. Spray a baking sheet with cooking spray.

4. Arrange cooked potatoes on the sheet and sprinkle with Cajun seasoning and salt.

5. Bake for 30 minutes. Then broil on low for 10 minutes to crispen.

Calories per serving: 146 – Fat: 0 – Sodium: 188 mg.
For exchange diets, count: 2 starch.
Preparation time: 10 minutes. – Microwave time: 8 minutes.
Baking time: 40 minutes.

Used with permission of the innkeepers at Mountain Creek Bed & Breakfast (see page 129)

MINI BAKED RED POTATOES
8 servings, 2 potatoes each

16 small red potatoes
1/2 cup broiled and drained bacon
crumbles

1 cup nonfat sour cream

1. Wash potatoes and pierce skins 4 times with a fork. Bake for 30 minutes at 350°, or microwave for 6 to 8 minutes, turning potatoes once during cooking.

2. When potatoes are tender, cut in half and carefully scoop out center with spoon or melon baller, leaving skin intact. Mix hot potatoes with bacon and sour cream in a medium mixing bowl.

3. Restuff potato mixture into potato skins and place on a baking pan. Reheat for 10 minutes at 350°. Serve immediately.

Calories per serving: 222 – Fat: 2 g. – Sodium: 127 mg.
For exchange diets, count: 2 starch, 1/2 skim milk.
Preparation time: 20 minutes. – Baking time: 30 minutes
or Microwave baking time: 8 minutes. – Reheating time: 10 minutes.

Used with permission of the innkeepers at Peacock Hill Country Inn (see page 71)

MISSY POTATOES

12 1/2-cup servings

nonstick cooking spray
2-pound package frozen hash brown
  potatoes, thawed
16-ounce carton nonfat sour cream
10 3/4-ounce can reduced-fat cream
  of celery soup
1 cup shredded reduced-fat sharp
  cheddar cheese

1 teaspoon salt
1 teaspoon coarsely ground black
  pepper
dash of Tabasco
8 reduced-fat cracked pepper crackers,
  crumbled

1. Preheat oven to 350°.

2. Spray a 13 x 9-inch baking dish with cooking spray.

3. Combine all ingredients except cracker crumbs in a large mixing bowl; spoon into baking dish.

4. Sprinkle cracker crumbs evenly over top of potato mixture. Bake for 40 minutes or until bubbly.

Calories per serving: 140 – Fat: 2 g. – Sodium: 339 mg.
For exchange diets, count: 2 starch.
Preparation time: 15 minutes. – Baking time: 40 minutes.

Used with permission of the innkeepers at The Park House

Camden Harbour Inn

Kerran & Joseph Ascoli, Innkeepers
83 Bayview Street
Camden, Maine 04843
(207) 236-4200;
Toll free: (800) 236-4266;
Fax: (207) 236-7063
E-mail: 73204.1222@compuserve.com
http://www.4chi.com

The Camden Harbour Inn, built in 1874, overlooks one of Maine's most historic and picturesque harbors. In the late 1800s the village of Camden was a working seaport bustling with cargo and fishing schooners. At that time steamships, traveling in the summer from Boston to Bangor, would lay over in Camden Harbor and passengers would disembark for overnight lodging at the inn. Imagine the best cuisine, and you will not be disappointed. The restaurant, Cetacea, offers the freshest seasonal foods available, which are skillfully prepared into distinctive regional and classic presentation. This recipe was developed by Chef Joseph Ascoli, a culinary graduate of Johnson and Wales University.

ROASTED RED BLISS POTATOES
WITH GARLIC & FETA DRESSING
8 servings

16 red bliss potatoes
1 tablespoon olive oil
1/2 teaspoon black pepper
1 teaspoon cayenne pepper
   or favorite spice mix
1/2 teaspoon salt
1 tablespoon fresh rosemary, finely diced

1 teaspoon fresh thyme leaves

DRESSING:
4 fresh garlic cloves
4 ounces feta cheese
dash of salt & pepper
1 tablespoon extra virgin olive oil

1. Preheat oven to 450°.

2. Wash the potatoes and cut them in half or in quarters and place on a baking sheet. Drizzle with olive oil and then sprinkle spices and herbs to coat. Roast until golden brown, but not so that they are completely done in the center, about 30 minutes.

3. Meanwhile, place the garlic cloves, cheese, and salt and pepper in a food processor and blend until all ingredients are well mixed. Then drizzle in the olive oil slowly until the mixture forms a smooth but firm paste. Taste for seasonings and adjust.

4. Remove potatoes from pan and mix with the dressing. Return to the baking sheet, and reheat for another 3 to 5 minutes or until the potatoes are warm and the dressing just begins to bubble. Serve immediately.

Calories per slice: 212 – Fat: 6 g. – Sodium: 299 mg.
For exchange diets, count: 1 1/2 starch, 1/2 skim milk, 1 fat.
Preparation time: 10 minutes. – Roasting time: 35 minutes.

Used with permission of the innkeepers at Camden Harbour Inn

The Park House

**Lynda & Joe Petty and
Susan Bentley, Innkeepers
888 Holland Street
Saugatuck, Michigan 49453
(616) 857-4535;
Toll free: (800) 321-4535**

Relive a bit of Saugatuck history at the Park House. Built in 1857 by lumberman H.D. Moore, the Park House is Saugatuck's oldest residence. For over a century, hospitality has existed in time-honored tradition. From Susan B. Anthony to the early Oxbow artists, guests of the Park House have enjoyed a cordial atmosphere and winsome surroundings. It's not far from the dunes and Lake Michigan.

SPATZLE
12 1/2-cup servings

4 cups flour
3 eggs or 3/4 cup liquid egg substitute
1 cup water
1 tablespoon salt

boiling water
1 cup grated reduced-fat Swiss cheese
Garnish: chopped green onions

1. Combine flour, eggs, water, and salt in a mixing bowl. Beat until very stiff, the dough is free of air pockets, and it does not stick to the side of the bowl.

2. Put manual spatzle strainer (available inexpensively at kitchen shops) over a pot of boiling salt water. Push small amounts of dough through the strainer into the water.

3. Skim off spatzle pasta pieces as they come to the top. Test for doneness and place in a large bowl. Alternate with layers of cheese. Serve hot with onion garnish.

Calories per serving: 200 – Fat: 3 g. – Sodium: 286 mg.
For exchange diets, count: 2 1/2 starch.
Preparation time: 15 minutes.

Used with permission of the innkeepers at Flemingsburg House Bed & Breakfast
at Sweetwater Farm (see page 6)

TYROLEAN DUMPLINGS
8 *dumplings*

8 slices bread
1/4 cup diced bacon, broiled crisp
  and drained
1 1/2 cups flour
1 cup skim milk
1/2 cup liquid egg substitute

1/2 teaspoon basil
1 teaspoon dried parsley
1 tablespoon farina or cream of wheat
  cereal
1/4 teaspoon salt
1/4 teaspoon pepper

1. Remove crusts from bread and cut into cubes.

2. Combine bread with all remaining ingredients and mix well. Allow mixture to stand for 15 minutes, then form dough into 8 round dumplings.

3. Cook dumplings in boiling salted water for 10 to 15 minutes until just cooked through. Serve as a side dish with red meat entrées.

Calories per serving: 195 – Fat: 3 g. – Sodium: 280 mg.
For exchange diets, count: 2 starch, 1/2 fat.
Preparation time: 15 minutes. – Standing time: 15 minutes.
Cooking time: 15 minutes.

Used with permission of the innkeepers at Flemingsburg House Bed & Breakfast
at Sweetwater Farm (see page 6)

Poipu Bed & Breakfast Inn

Dotti Cichou, Innkeeper
2720 Hoonani Road
Poipu Beach (Kauai), Hawaii 96756
(808) 742-1146;
Toll free: (800) 552-0095 & (800) 22-POIPU;
Fax: (808) 742-6843
e-mail: poipu@aloha.net

Experience another time and place at a unique plantation style accommodation on the sunny south shore of the Garden Island of Kauai at the Poipu Bed & Breakfast. Built in 1933, the original plantation house of the Poipu B & B has been lovingly renovated to preserve the charm and elegance of old Hawaii while providing for every modern luxury. Sample fresh exotic fruits, tropical fruit juices, a variety of toasts with tropical jams and jellies, a choice of coffees and exotic teas, as well as locally baked Hawaiian sweet bread, macadamia nut muffins, or Dotti's favorite of bagels & cream cheese with papaya salsa. By request, guests can have breakfast served to them in bed!

Little Tree Bed & Breakfast

Charles and Kay Giddens, Innkeepers
P.O. Drawer II
Taos, New Mexico 87571
(505) 776-8467;
Toll free: (800) 334-8467
E-mail: little@taos.newmex.com

Little Tree is a place to slow down and enjoy the quiet of the country. From the patio seating area in the courtyard of this authentic adobe hacienda, you have eastward views of Taos Mountain, northward views of Valdez and Gallina, and westward views of the mesa and fabulous sunsets. Upon arrival you will find homemade cookies in your room, and complementary drinks and snacks are available. Breakfast of gourmet coffee and freshly prepared food is served from 8:00 to 9:00 a.m.

BREAKFAST PASTA
8 1-cup servings

8 ounces spaghetti
6 fresh mushrooms
4 green onions
2 cloves garlic
1 teaspoon olive oil
6 eggs

2 Roma tomatoes
1 tablespoon margarine
1/2 cup finely grated Parmesan cheese
1 1/2 teaspoons chopped fresh basil
2 tablespoons fresh parsley
freshly ground black pepper

1. Cook pasta in boiling water for 8 minutes or per package instructions.

2. While pasta is cooking, slice mushrooms and green onions. Crush garlic.

3. In a large skillet, sauté garlic and mushrooms in olive oil. Before mushrooms are thoroughly cooked, add green onions. Remove from heat and reserve for later use.

4. Crack eggs into bowl and beat lightly.

5. Dice tomatoes into 1-inch cubes.

6. When pasta is cooked, drain. In large skillet melt margarine; add pasta to skillet and stir briefly. Add eggs and half of Parmesan cheese. Stir until eggs begin to form curds on pasta. Then add garlic, mushrooms, green onions, basil, and parsley.

7. Add chopped tomatoes, stirring briefly to incorporate. Immediately place on serving plates and sprinkle with fresh ground black pepper and rest of cheese.

Calories per serving: 161 – Fat: 4 g. – Sodium: 132 mg.
For exchange diets, count: 1 starch, 1 vegetable, 1 lean meat.
Preparation time: 20 minutes.

Used with permission of the innkeepers at Little Tree Bed & Breakfast

CHEESE TORTELLINI WITH NUTTY HERB SAUCE
8 1-cup servings

1 pound ricotta-filled fresh
  or dried tortellini or ravioli
1/4 cup walnuts
1 tablespoon margarine
1/4 cup pine nuts, chopped

2 tablespoons chopped fresh parsley
2 teaspoons fresh thyme
salt and pepper to taste
1/4 cup nonfat ricotta cheese
1/4 cup evaporated skim milk

1. Add the pasta to a large pan of rapidly boiling water and cook just until tender. Drain and return to pan.

2. While pasta is cooking, chop walnuts into small pieces. Heat margarine in a heavy saucepan over medium heat until foaming. Add walnuts and pine nuts and stir for 5 minutes or until golden brown. Add the parsley, thyme, salt, and pepper.

3. In a small bowl, beat the ricotta with the evaporated skim milk. Add to saucepan and warm through. Add the nutty herb sauce to the pasta and toss well to combine. Top with a dollop of ricotta cream. Serve immediately.

Calories per serving: 234 – Fat: 10 g. (To reduce fat, use fewer nuts).
Sodium: 168 mg.
For exchange diets, count: 1 starch, 1 skim milk, 1 1/2 fat.
Preparation time: 15 minutes.

Used with permission of the innkeepers at Milton House Bed & Breakfast Inn (see page 161)

✳ ✳ ✳

Soups

STRAWBERRY CHAMPAGNE SOUP

6 3/4-cup servings

2 tablespoons cornstarch
1/2 cup cold water
10-ounce package frozen strawberries
in syrup, thawed
1 cup 50% less fat sour cream

2 cups evaporated skim milk
2-4 tablespoons strawberry liqueur
champagne
whipped cream
strawberries

1. Dissolve cornstarch in cold water. Bring strawberries to a boil in a small saucepan, then stir in cornstarch mixture. Stir and simmer for three minutes. Transfer to a large bowl and cool to room temperature. To speed chilling, place in the refrigerator for 30 minutes.

2. Gently whisk in sour cream, evaporated milk, and liqueur. Cover and chill until ready to serve.

3. Pour soup into individual clear-glass footed bowls or large wine goblets. Add a splash of champagne to each bowl, and garnish with whipped cream and a strawberry.

Calories per serving: 213 – Fat: 4 g. – Sodium: 129 mg.
For exchange diets, count: 2 fruit, 1 skim milk.
Preparation time: 15 minutes. – Chilling time: 30 minutes.

Used with permission of the innkeepers at Rosewood Country Inn (see page 92)

GAZPACHO
8 3/4-cup servings

2 cups fresh or canned tomato wedges
1/2 cup finely chopped green peppers
1/2 cup finely chopped celery
1/2 cup finely chopped cucumber
1/4 cup finely chopped onion
2 teaspoons snipped parsley
1 teaspoon snipped chives

1 small clove garlic, minced
3 tablespoons tarragon wine vinegar
2 tablespoons olive oil
1/4 teaspoon black pepper
1 teaspoon Worcestershire sauce
3 cups tomato juice
1 teaspoon salt (optional)

1. Combine all ingredients in a glass or stainless steel bowl.

2. Cover and chill at least 2 hours or overnight.

Calories per serving: 48 – Fat: 2 g. – Sodium: 608 mg. with salt. (333 mg. without salt.)
(To further reduce sodium, use no-added-salt tomato juice.)
For exchange diets, count: 2 vegetables.
Preparation time: 15 minutes. Chilling time: at least 2 hours.

Used with permission of the innkeepers at Little Warren Bed & Breakfast

Little Warren Bed & Breakfast

Patsy & Tom Miller, Innkeepers
304 East Park Avenue
Tarboro, North Carolina 27886
(919) 823-1314;
Toll free: (800) 309-1314

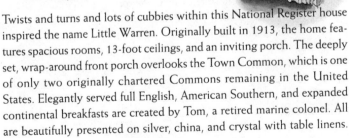

Twists and turns and lots of cubbies within this National Register house inspired the name Little Warren. Originally built in 1913, the home features spacious rooms, 13-foot ceilings, and an inviting porch. The deeply set, wrap-around front porch overlooks the Town Common, which is one of only two originally chartered Commons remaining in the United States. Elegantly served full English, American Southern, and expanded continental breakfasts are created by Tom, a retired marine colonel. All are beautifully presented on silver, china, and crystal with table linens.

BROCCOLI CHEESE SOUP

12 1 1/2-cup servings

1 tablespoon soft margarine
3/4 cup chopped onion
6 cups water
6 low-sodium chicken bouillon cubes
8 ounces fine egg noodles
1/4 teaspoon salt

2 10-ounce packages chopped broccoli
1/8 teaspoon garlic powder
6 cups skim milk
8 ounces shredded reduced-fat
  American cheese
pepper to taste

1. In a large stockpot, sauté onion in margarine for 3 minutes. Add water and bouillon cubes. Heat to boiling until cubes are dissolved. Gradually add noodles and salt. Heat till mixture boils, then boil uncovered for 3 minutes.

2. Stir in broccoli and garlic powder and cook for 4 minutes. Add milk, cheese, and pepper. Continue cooking till cheese melts, stirring constantly.

3. Serve hot. This recipe an be frozen and reheated in double boiler.

Calories per serving: 185 – Fat: 5 g. – Sodium: 358 mg.
For exchange diets, count: 1 skim milk, 1 vegetable, 1/2 starch, 1 fat.
Preparation time: 20 minutes.

Used with permission of the innkeepers at The Serendipity House

The Serendipity House

Terry & Paula Endicott, Innkeepers
S. Highway 287
P.O. Box 1132
Dumas, Texas 79029
(806) 935-0339;
Toll free: (800) 839-7869

Comfort, elegance, and hospitality all come together under one roof at the Serendipity House. After a good night's rest, a hearty breakfast, prepared by owners Paula and Terry Endicott, will be waiting in the dining room. Weather permitting, guests may also eat on the deck for a better view of the neighboring canyon. From this vantage point early risers can catch a breath-taking sunrise. The morning menu includes egg casserole, biscuits and croissants, fruit, juice, and coffee. But the highlight of the meal is sure to be the gourmet jams and jellies made on site by Paula. Varieties include a not so ordinary grape, pungent wine, delicate apple-cinnamon, and zippy jalepeño, all of which are official "Taste of Texas" foods. A complimentary jar of jelly is included in each room's guest basket, which is also stocked with extra necessities and sundries.

NORWEGIAN FRUIT SOUP

8 3/4-cup servings

4 cups water
8 ounces mixed dried fruits
1/4 cup golden raisins
1 stick cinnamon
2 tablespoons lemon juice

2 tablespoons orange juice
1/2 cup sugar
1/4 teaspoon salt
1/4 cup minute tapioca

1. Bring water to a boil in a medium saucepan. Add fruit and raisins and simmer for 20 minutes.

2. Add all remaining ingredients and cook for 10 minutes or until tapioca is transparent. Serve hot or cold. Remove cinnamon stick before serving.

Calories per serving: 157 – Fat: 0 – Sodium: 70 mg.
For exchange diets, count: 2 1/2 fruit.
Preparation time: 5 minutes. – Cooking time: 30 minutes.

Used with permission of the innkeepers at Eagles' Landing Bed and Breakfast (see page 52)

Milton House Bed & Breakfast Inn

John & Karin Tipton, Innkeepers
113 West Main Street
Stanley, Virginia 22851
(540) 778-2495;
Toll free: (800) 816-3731;
Fax: (540) 778-3451
E-mail: milhouse@shentel.net

Milton House Bed & Breakfast Inn is a unique 1915 southern colonial home located in the bucolic town of Stanley in the Shenandoah Valley near Luray Caverns, Virginia. The house was ordered from the Sears "Big Book" catalogue, in which "Milton" was the name of the floor plan. This Inn has a three-diamond award from AAA. Culinary artistry is performed by Karin with special German cuisine or low-fat meals available upon request. Breakfast is as delicious as it is hearty, and guests indulge in cakes or cookies in the afternoon along with a heart-warming pot of tea or frosty glass of lemonade.

TORTELLINI SOUP

8 1-cup servings

1/2 cup chopped onion
nonstick cooking spray
46-ounce can vegetable juice
2 cups water
2 no-added-salt chicken bouillon cubes
10-ounce package frozen spinach
2 carrots, chopped

1 teaspoon sugar
1/4 teaspoon seasoned salt
1/2 teaspoon oregano
1/2 teaspoon basil
8-ounce package dry tortellini with
   Parmesan cheese

1. Sauté onion in a no-stick skillet that has been sprayed with cooking spray. Add vegetable juice, water, bouillon, frozen block of spinach, carrots, sugar, salt, and seasonings. Bring to a boil. Turn heat to medium and simmer for 15 minutes.

2. Bring to a boil again and add tortellini. Simmer another 30 minutes.

> Calories per serving: 140 – Fat: 3 g. – Sodium: 832 mg.
> For exchange diets, count: 1 starch, 1 lean meat.
> Preparation time: 15 minutes. – Cooking time: 45 minutes.

Used with permission of the innkeepers at Doll House Inn Historical Bed & Breakfast (see page 61)

The Brass Lantern Inn

Andy Aldrich, Innkeeper
717 Maple Street
Stowe, Vermont 05672
(802) 253-2229;
Toll free: (800) 729-2980;
Fax: (802) 253-7425
E-mail: brasslntrn@aol.com

The Brass Lantern was recently named a Country Inn of Distinction and received the Golden Fork Award by the Gourmet Diner's Society of North America. The country breakfast at the Brass Lantern is always a treat. Everything served is prepared fresh daily—including the breads and desserts—using only Vermont seal-of-quality products and produce. Each afternoon and into the evening enjoy complimentary coffee, tea, hot chocolate, and home-baked goodies by a crackling fire in our living room or out on the patio as the sun slips behind Mount Mansfield. The Brass Lantern Inn is located on the edge of Stowe Village. Restored by Innkeeper Andy Aldrich and his son, Dustin, the inn's wide-planked floors, exposed beams, stenciled walls, and antique furnishings provide character to this romantic getaway.

BUTTERNUT SQUASH SOUP
12 1-cup servings

1 large butternut squash, washed, peeled, seeded, and chunked
2 cups water
1 teaspoon salt
1/2 cup diced celery
1/2 cup diced onions
1/2 cup diced green bell peppers
1 tablespoon melted margarine
1/4 cup white wine

1 teaspoon tarragon leaves
1/2 teaspoon ground cinnamon
1/2 teaspoon ground nutmeg
1/4 teaspoon ground cloves
4 cups no-added-salt chicken stock
1/4 cup all-purpose flour
1 tablespoon melted margarine
1/2 cup Vermont maple syrup
1/4 cup dry sherry

1. Place squash in a large saucepan with salt and water, and cook until soft (approximately 30 minutes). Or microwave the squash with water and salt on high power for 15 to 18 minutes until tender.

2. Strain out the squash and transfer to a blender container with half of the liquid; reserve the other half of the liquid.

3. In a stockpot, sauté the diced vegetables in margarine and wine for 5 minutes. Add the herbs and spices. Add the chicken stock and 1 cup of reserved liquid.

4. In a mixing bowl, blend flour with margarine.

5. Bring vegetable mixture to a boil, then whisk in margarine and flour.

6. Puree the cooked squash in the blender. Add to the pot and cook on low heat for 5 minutes, stirring often. Add the syrup and sherry. Mix well and serve.

Calories per serving: 97 – Fat: 2 g. – Sodium: 213 mg.
For exchange diets, count: 1 starch.
Preparation time: 20 minutes. Cooking time: 45 minutes on stovetop, or 30 with microwave and stovetop.

Used with permission of the innkeeper at The Brass Lantern Inn

Green Springs Plantation Bed & Breakfast

Madeline Nevill, Innkeeper
7463 Tunica Trace
St. Francisville, Louisiana 70775
(504) 635-4232;
Toll free: (800) 457-4978;
Fax: (504) 635-3355

Green Springs Plantation Bed & Breakfast is located four miles north of beautiful St. Francisville, Louisiana. This gracious country estate sits in a peaceful garden setting on land that was once part of the huge Spanish land grant deeded to the Barrow family in 1795. Every morning guests are served a hot plantation breakfast with fresh fruit of the season, scrambled eggs with chopped parsley, buttered grits, finger sausages, hot homemade biscuits, pear preserves, and lots of coffee or tea.

CRABMEAT AND CORN BISQUE
4 1 1/2-cup servings

1 tablespoon soft margarine
1/2 cup all-purpose flour
1/2 quart crab stock or no-added-salt chicken stock
6-ounce package frozen corn or kernels from 2 large ears fresh sweet corn

3/4 cup evaporated skim milk
1/2 pound flaked crabmeat
salt and pepper to taste
3/4 cup finely chopped green onions

1. Melt margarine in a 5-quart saucepan; add flour and stir until flour begins to stick to pan. Add stock; bring to boil, stirring constantly, then simmer 15 minutes. Add corn and simmer 15 minutes more.

2. Pour in milk and stir well. Gently add crabmeat. Remove from heat and let stand 15 minutes for flavors to blend.

3. Refrigerate and serve later, or reheat gently to serving temperature. Season to taste. Just before serving, add green onions.

Calories per serving: 231 – Fat: 4 g. – Sodium: 768 mg.
For exchange diets, count: 2 very lean meat, 1 starch, 1 skim milk.
Preparation time: 15 minutes. Cooking time: 30 minutes. Standing time: 15 minutes.

Used with permission of the innkeeper at Green Springs Plantation Bed & Breakfast

Red Clover Inn

Sue & Harris Zuckerman, Innkeepers
7 Woodward Road
Mendon, Vermont 05701
(802) 775-2290;
Toll free: (800) 752-0571;
Fax: (802) 773-0594
E-mail: redclovr@vermontel.com

Nestled on 13 rolling acres, surrounded by the Green Mountains, the Red Clover Inn offers guests a relaxed, inviting atmosphere, beautiful rooms, and some of the finest gourmet fare. This farmhouse inn was built in about 1849 by the Ripley family of Rutland, Vermont, who used the farm as a summer retreat. A full country breakfast is served year-round. There is always fresh fruit, juice, and scrumptious highlights such as Cinnamon Swirl French Toast or Apple Pecan Pancakes with locally-made warmed maple syrup.

CURRIED CARROT SOUP

4 1 1/2-cup servings

1 tablespoon olive oil
1 medium onion, chopped
2 stalks celery, chopped
1 pound carrots, peeled and chopped
1 small red pepper, chopped
1/2 teaspoon red curry paste
   (optional)

1 1/2 teaspoons curry powder
2 cups no-added-salt chicken stock
1 cup evaporated skim milk
salt and white pepper to taste

1. In a stockpot, sauté onion and celery in oil until softened. Add carrots and pepper. Sauté briefly. Add curry paste and curry powder. Add stock and bring to a boil. Cover and simmer until vegetables are very tender, about 20 minutes.

2. Purée in a blender and put through a sieve.

3. Return to pan over medium heat. Add milk and season with salt and pepper.

Calories per serving: 130 – Fat: 3 g. sodium: 136 mg.
For exchange diets, count: 4 vegetables, 1/2 fat.
Preparation time: 10 minutes. – Cooking time: 20 minutes.

Used with permission of the innkeepers at Red Clover Inn

RED LENTIL SOUP
4 1 1/2-cup servings

1 medium onion, chopped fine
1 red or green bell pepper,
   chopped fine
2 gloves garlic, minced
1 tablespoon soft margarine
1 quart no-added-salt chicken stock,
   boiling

2 tomatoes, peeled, seeded,
   and chopped
1 cup red lentils, picked over and rinsed
Optional: crumbled crisp bacon
   or bits of lean ham
salt, pepper, lemon juice, cumin,
   and paprika (use none, any, or all)

1. Sauté onion, pepper, and garlic in margarine until soft and translucent. Add boiling stock, tomatoes, lentils, and optional bacon.

2. Simmer 1 1/2 to 2 hours, stirring fairly often. Add water if necessary. Season to taste with any or all of the following: salt, pepper, lemon juice, cumin, and paprika.

Calories per serving: 211 – Fat: 3 g. – Sodium: 49 mg.
For exchange diets, count: 1 lean meat, 2 starch.
Preparation time: 10 minutes. Cooking time: 2 hours.

Used with permission of the innkeepers at The Chipman Inn

The Chipman Inn

Joyce Henderson & Bill Pierce, Innkeepers
Route 125
Ripton, Vermont 05766
(802) 388-2390;
Toll free: (800) 890-2390;
Fax: (802) 388-2390
E-mail: smudge@together.net

Located in the heart of the Green Mountains of central Vermont, the lovely, tranquil setting of the inn matches its informal atmosphere where coziness and elegance combine for a peaceful retreat to get away and refresh. Outdoor activities are many and varied. Vermont's Long Trail, as well as many other scenic walks and back country roads, provides an opportunity to enjoy the unspoiled landscape.

TOMATO FLORENTINE SOUP

8 1-cup servings

nonstick cooking spray
1 large onion, chopped
1 large clove garlic, chopped
28-ounce can chunky crushed tomatoes
10-ounce package frozen spinach,
   defrosted and minced in blender
   or food processor

1 large green bell pepper, diced
2 teaspoons dried basil
1 teaspoon dried oregano

1. Spray a large stockpot with cooking spray. Add onions and garlic and sauté until tender.

2. Add remaining ingredients and simmer for 20 minutes or until it smells so good you can't wait any more. Add salt and pepper to taste.

Calories per serving: 68 – Fat: 0 – Sodium: 616 mg.
(To reduce sodium, use no-added-salt chunky tomatoes.)
For exchange diets, count: 3 vegetable.
Preparation time: 10 minutes. – Cooking time: 20 minutes.

Used with permission of the innkeepers at The Brewster Inn

The Brewster Inn

Ivy & Michael Brooks, Innkeepers
37 Zions Hill Road
Dexter, Maine 04930
(207) 924-3130
E-mail: brooksmj@voicenet.com

Featuring comfortable, classic 1930s elegance
in a small-town setting, the Brewster Inn offers a warm, relaxing, and friendly atmosphere. Built for Governor Ralph Owen Brewster by noted architect John Calvin Stevens, this Historic Register home features white siding and a slate roof set off by spacious gardens and an ornamental pond. Guests may use the dining room, living room, sun room, and conservatory, which are furnished in a variety of antiques, reproductions, and family heirlooms. Books abound, as do art and craft objects, and an antique radio collection spills over into many of the rooms.

Meat, Fish, and Poultry

DUBLIN BROIL

8 4-ounce servings

1 flank steak (2 to 2 1/2 pounds)
2 teaspoons unseasoned meat tenderizer
2 tablespoons dry sherry
2 tablespoons Worcestershire sauce

1 tablespoon sugar
1 teaspoon salt
1 tablespoon honey

1. Pierce surface of steak at 1-inch intervals with sharp fork.

2. Combine remaining ingredients in a small bowl and pour over steak. Cover and refrigerate for 1 hour or more, turning occasionally.

3. Place steak on broiler pan about 3 inches from heat, and broil 3 minutes on each side. To serve, slice thinly with sharp knife, carving at an angle against the grain.

Calories per serving: 190 – Fat: 8 g. – Sodium: 814 mg.
(To reduce sodium, omit salt and use less meat tenderizer.)
Preparation time: 10 minutes. – Marinating time: 1 hour.
Broiling time: 6 minutes.

Used with permission of the innkeepers at Liberty Hill Inn Bed and Breakfast

Liberty Hill Inn Bed and Breakfast

Jack & Beth Flanagan, Innkeepers
77 Main Street (Route 6A)
Yarmouth Port, Massachusetts 02675
(508) 362-3976;
Toll free: (800) 821-3977

This elegant bed and breakfast inn is located on Cape Cod's historic Old Kings Highway, and is on the National Register of Historic Places. Guests may want privilege to reflect on the words of President John F. Kennedy: "Whenever I have to make an important decision, I always go to the Cape and walk the beaches."

MARINATED BEEF TENDERLOIN
12 4-ounce servings

1 cup port wine
1 cup soy sauce
2 tablespoons olive oil
3 cloves garlic, chopped
1 teaspoon fresh thyme, or
    1 teaspoon dried thyme

1 teaspoon fresh ground black pepper
1 teaspoon hot sauce
4 pounds trimmed beef tenderloin

1. Combine first seven ingredients and pour over beef. Marinate covered 4 to 8 hours, turning once.

2. Preheat charcoal broiler and preheat oven to 325°.

3. Remove beef from marinade. Brown tenderloin under broiler for 3 minutes on all sides.

4. Place in baking pan and bake 1 1/2 hours or until meat thermometer reads 140°.

5. Slice tenderloin to desired thickness and serve.

Calories per 4-ounce portion: 179 – Fat: 8 g. – Sodium: 54 mg.
For exchange diets, count: 3 lean meat.
Preparation time: 10 minutes. – Marinating time: 4 hours.
Roasting time: 1 1/2 hours.

Used with permission of the innkeeper at Buckhorn Inn (see page 73)

Brierley Hill Country Inn

Barry & Carole Speton, Innkeepers
Route 2, Box 21A Borden Road
Lexington, Virginia 24450
(540) 464-8421;
Toll free: (800) 422-4925;
Fax: (540) 464-8925
E-mail: cspeton@cfw.com
http://www.brierleyhill.com

While guests revel in the magnificent sunrise views of the Blue Ridge Mountains and Shenandoah Valley from this country home, innkeeper Carole transfers tomatoes, peppers, herbs, and strawberries from garden to kitchen. Brierley Hill becomes filled with the fragrance of coffee and a gourmet breakfast in the making. In the large dining room, a cheery fire warms guests seated at separate tables. A graduate of La Varenne Cooking School at the Greenbrier Resort in West Virginia, Carole also prepares a four-course dinner, a set menu, on Thursday, Friday, and Saturday.

PORK CONFIT WITH ONION MARMALADE
4 servings

1 pound pork loin roast
1/2 head green cabbage
2 medium onions, thinly sliced
1/2 teaspoon olive oil
1/4 cup balsamic vinegar

1/4 cup sherry
1/4 cup diced dried dates
1 medium apple, peeled and diced
chicken stock as required
1/2 teaspoon olive oil

1. Roast a pork loin roast at 350° for 1 1/2 hours, or pan-sauté sliced pork tenderloin until cooked through.

2. Meanwhile, slice cabbage into strips. Blanch in boiling water for 2 minutes; drain and reserve.

3. Sauté onion in olive oil until soft. Add vinegar, sherry, dates, and apples, and cook until fruit is soft. Add chicken stock if necessary to obtain desired consistency.

4. When pork is cooked through, cook the blanched cabbage slices in a little olive oil until soft but still crunchy.

5. To serve, mound cooked cabbage on plate, fan pork slices over cabbage, and top with onion marmalade. Garnish with parsley or a sprig of fresh sage.

Calories per serving: 324 – Fat: 14 g. – Sodium: 64 mg.
For exchange diets, count: 4 lean meat, 1 fruit, 1 vegetable.
Preparation time: 10 minutes. – Roasting time: 1 1/2 hours.

Used with permission of the innkeepers at Brierley Hill Country Inn (see previous page)

MARINATED LAMB
4 3-ounce servings

2 tablespoons vegetable oil
1/4 cup red wine vinegar
1/4 cup lemon juice
1 minced garlic clove

1 teaspoon crushed dried rosemary
1 teaspoon dried oregano
salt and pepper to taste
1 pound boned leg or shoulder of lamb

1. Combine first seven ingredients in a bowl or zippered plastic bag.

2. Add meat and let marinate in refrigerator 4 to 6 hours, turning meat over several times.

3. Remove meat from marinade. Cut into chunks for shish-kabobs or grill whole over medium flame for 6 to 8 minutes per side or until desired doneness.

Calories per serving: 245 – Fat: 15 g. – Sodium: 71 mg.
For exchange diets count: 3 1/2 lean meat, 1 fat.
Preparation time: 10 minutes. – Marinating time: 4 hours.
Grilling time: 16 minutes.

Used with permission of the innkeeper at Dakota Shepherd Bed & Breakfast

Dakota Shepherd Bed & Breakfast

Sheryl Trohkimoinen, Innkeeper
RR 3, Box 25C
Vale, South Dakota 57788
(605) 456-2836;
Fax: (605) 892-6007

Experience country life at its best on an authentic sheep farm/ranch. Enjoy spring lambs, summer gardens, harvest's bounty, or winter's quiet. Ride a horse-drawn wagon, watch a sheep-dog demonstration, or visit nearby Black Hills attractions and hiking trails in Bear Butte State Park. Delicious homemade breakfasts are served family style. This modern home with a comfortable veranda offers peaceful opportunities for star gazing, "birding," or enjoying the panoramic landscape. You'll enjoy 1940s furnishings, family heirlooms in pretty, spacious bedrooms tastefully decorated with handmade quilts, and delicate handiwork. Families appreciate the cozy two-bedroom suite.

FISH KABOBS
8 4-ounce servings

2 1/2 pounds assorted fish cut in 2-inch cubes (cod, shrimp, swordfish, scallops, salmon)
2 large onions, cut in wedges
1 pound mushrooms, cleaned and stemmed
1 pound cherry tomatoes, washed
16-ounce bottle Newman's Own Italian dressing

1. Alternate pieces of fish on a skewer with pieces of onion, mushrooms, and cherry tomatoes. This will fill about 16 long skewers. Place in a glass pan.

2. Pour dressing over kabobs, cover, and marinate 2 to 3 hours in the refrigerator. Remove from pan and grill over charcoal fire about 10 minutes, turning a few times during cooking.

Calories per serving: 120 – Fat: 6 g. – Sodium: 400 mg.
(To reduce sodium, use less salad dressing.)
For exchange diets, count: 3 very lean meat, 1/2 fat.
Preparation time: 5 minutes. – Marinating time: 2–3 hours.
Grilling time: 10 minutes.

Used with permission of the innkeepers at Liberty Hill Inn Bed and Breakfast (see page 170)

FISH VERACRUZ

6 servings

1 tablespoon oil
4 cloves garlic, chopped
1/2 cup finely chopped onion
2 pounds tomatoes, peeled
  and finely chopped
1 green bell pepper, cut into strips
1/2 teaspoon salt
1/2 teaspoon pepper
2 bay leaves

1 teaspoon oregano
2 tablespoons chopped green olives
1/4 cup capers
nonstick cooking spray
6 4-ounce fillets of a firm, mild fish
  (sea bass, red snapper, catfish)
1/4 teaspoon salt
1/2 teaspoon pepper

1. For sauce: heat oil in large saucepan. Add garlic and onion; sauté for about 3 minutes. Add the tomatoes and bring to a boil. Add the bell pepper and stir for 2 minutes. Add salt, pepper, bay leaves, and oregano. Return to a boil, cover, and cook on low heat for about 8 minutes. Add olives and capers, and cook another 5 minutes. Correct seasonings; remove from heat. Remove bay leaves and set mixture aside.

2. Twenty minutes before serving, preheat the oven to 375°. Rinse the fish fillets and pat dry; season with salt and pepper.

3. Spray a baking dish with nonstick cooking spray. Place fillets in the baking dish. Spoon sauce to completely cover the fillets. Cover pan with aluminum foil and bake 10 to 15 minutes or until fish just begins to flake.

Calories per serving: 254 – Fat: 8 g. – Sodium: 435 mg.
For exchange diets, count: 6 lean meat, 2 vegetable.
Preparation time: 15 minutes. – Baking time: 15 minutes.

Used with permission of the innkeepers at The Inn at Merridun

The Inn at Merridun

Peggy & Jim Waller, Innkeepers
100 Merridun Place
Union, South Carolina 29379
(864) 427-7052

The Inn at Merridun is an elegant, yet comfortable antebellum mansion that has been lovingly restored to a one-of-a-kind country inn. It's city close—only a five minute walk from downtown Union, yet country quiet—the Inn is located in the center of 9 wooded acres. You will sense the hospitality as you stroll up to the marbled verandas beneath white Corinthian columns.

CHINOOK SALMON ON THE BARBECUE GRILL
4 servings

2 pounds Chinook salmon fillets, cut in large pieces, leave the skin on
non-irradiated seafood seasoning
lemon pepper seasoning

veggie pepper seasoning, preferably Salutes brand
fresh lemon wedges

1. Preheat grill to 400°.

2. Place the salmon fillets on the grill, skin side down. This will not be turned.

3. Season with seafood, lemon pepper, and veggie pepper seasoning.

4. Turn the grill down to medium low. Put lid down and cook for 20 minutes. Meat should be flaky tender.

5. Serve with wedges of fresh lemon.

Calories per serving: 236 – Fat: 7 g. – Sodium: 98 mg.
For exchange diets, count: 7 very lean meat. – Grilling time: 20 minutes.

Used with permission of the innkeeper at Wheeler on the Bay Lodge and Marina

CHICKEN BREASTS GLAZED
WITH SWEET MARMALADE
4 servings, 1 chicken breast each

1 tablespoon olive oil
1 egg or 1/4 cup liquid egg substitute
4 boneless and skinless chicken
  breast halves, pounded to 1/4 inch
  thickness
1/2 cup bread crumbs

GLAZE:
1/4 cup Grand Marnier
1/4 cup orange marmalade
1 teaspoon fresh lemon juice
1/4 teaspoon Worcestershire sauce
1/4 teaspoon Dijon mustard
1/4 teaspoon minced garlic

1. Heat olive oil in a medium skillet over medium-high heat.

2. Beat egg in shallow bowl. Dip chicken in egg, then in bread crumbs to coat. Cook in skillet 2 to 4 minutes per side.

3. Combine ingredients for glaze and spread over chicken. Reduce heat to low and continue cooking 4 to 5 minutes or until glaze color is dulled.

Calories per serving: 290 – Fat: 7 g. – Sodium: 176 mg.
For exchange diets, count: 4 lean meat, 1 fruit.
Preparation time: 15 minutes.

*Used with permission of the innkeepers at Whispering Pines Bed & Breakfast
on Atwood Lake (see page 83)*

TERIYAKI CHICKEN ON THE BARBECUE GRILL
4 servings

2 whole boneless chicken breasts,
  skin removed, cut in half

teriyaki sauce
Salt-free all-purpose seasoning

1. Preheat grill to 400°.

2. Place the chicken breasts on the grill.

3. Season with teriyaki sauce and all-purpose seasoning.

4. Turn the grill down to medium low. Put lid down and cook for 15 minutes. Turn chicken and season again. Cook 10 more minutes.

Calories per serving: 145 – Fat: 3 g. – Sodium: 235 mg.
For exchange diets, count: 4 very lean meat. – Grilling time: 25 minutes.

Used with permission of the innkeeper at Wheeler on the Bay Lodge and Marina (see page 175)

INNKEEPERS' WILD RICE AND CHICKEN DINNER
8 1-cup servings

1 package long grain and wild rice mix
13-ounce can reduced-fat cream of celery soup
2/3 cup skim milk
1/2 cup reduced-fat mayonnaise
1 tablespoon chopped onion
8-ounce can sliced water chestnuts, drained

4-ounce can sliced mushrooms, drained
10-ounce package frozen French-cut green beans
1 tablespoon diced fresh rosemary
2 cups diced cooked chicken
2 1/2 cups herb-seasoned stuffing mix
1 tablespoon melted margarine
1/2 cup fat-free chicken broth

1. Preheat oven to 350°.

2. Prepare rice mix according to directions using water, white wine, dark beer, or fat-free chicken broth.

3. Combine soup, milk, mayonnaise, onion, water chestnuts, mushrooms, green beans, and rosemary in a bowl. Fold in the chicken.

4. Spray a 9 x 13-inch baking dish with nonstick cooking spray.

5. Combine prepared rice with soup and chicken mixture in the prepared baking dish.

6. In a medium bowl, toss stuffing mix with margarine and broth. Sprinkle over the chicken. This may be frozen at this point or baked.

7. Bake for 25 to 30 minutes.

Calories per serving: 286 – Fat: 8 g. – Sodium: 442 mg.
For exchange diets, count: 2 lean meat, 2 starch, 1 vegetable.
Preparation time: 20 minutes. – Baking time: 30 minutes.

Used with permission of the innkeepers at King's Inn at Georgetown Bed & Breakfast (see page 29)

SESAME CHICKEN PASTA SALAD

8 1 1/2-cup servings

1 cup broccoli florets
6 ounces pasta spirals
1/4 cup sesame seeds
1 tablespoon olive oil
1 tablespoon sesame oil
1/3 cup soy sauce
1/3 cup rice vinegar

3 tablespoons sugar
1/2 teaspoon salt
1/2 teaspoon pepper
3 cups cooked, diced chicken breast
1/2 cup minced parsley
1 bunch sliced green onions

1. Blanch broccoli florets by placing in boiling water and cooking 3 minutes until tender crisp.

2. Cook pasta according to package directions, and drain well.

3. Toss broccoli and pasta together with all remaining ingredients in a large salad bowl, and serve with a chilled fruity white wine.

Calories per serving: 320 – Fat: 8 g. – Sodium: 691 mg.
For exchange diets, count: 2 starch, 3 lean meat.
Preparation time: 20 minutes.

Used with permission of the innkeeper at Holly Hill House Bed & Breakfast

Holly Hill House Bed & Breakfast

Lynne Sterling, Innkeeper
611 Polk Street
Port Townsend, Washington 98368
(360) 385-5619;
Toll free: (800) 435-1454 (out of state only)
E-mail: hollyhill@olympus.net

Step back in time to the elegant Victorian era by visiting the Holly Hill House, nestled in the heart of fascinating uptown Historic Port Townsend. Known as the Robert C. Hill House, this house was built in 1872 and is an example of intricate old-world craftsmanship reflecting the rich history of Washington's Victorian seaport. A sumptuous breakfast is prepared in the large country kitchen, then served with a gracious air in the formal dining room, accompanied by beautiful classical music.

SWEET AND SPICY MUSTARD
12 servings, 1 1/2 teaspoons each

4 tablespoons Grey Poupon
Dijon mustard

2 tablespoons honey or
apricot preserves

1. Mix mustard with honey or preserves in a bowl and serve with Spinach Pom Poms (see page 18) or as a condiment for grilled meats.

Calories per serving: 15 – Fat: 0 – Sodium: 65 mg.
For exchange diets, count: free.
Preparation time: 5 minutes.

Used with permission of the innkeepers at The Chestnut House Bed & Breakfast (see page 18)

Salads and
Vegetables

LEMON VEGETABLE MOLDED SALAD

8 servings

2 cups tomato juice
2 3-ounce packages regular or
   sugar-free lemon gelatin
1 cup diced celery
1 cup diced cucumber
1/2 cup chopped green pepper

2 tablespoons chopped onion
1 tablespoon horseradish
1/4 cup nonfat sour cream
1 cup nonfat salad dressing
   (Miracle Whip free)

1. Heat tomato juice in a saucepan. Bring to a boil and add gelatin, stirring to completely dissolve gelatin. Set aside to cool.

2. Place mixture in the refrigerator for 1 hour to thicken (it should lump on a spoon like pudding), then fold in the remaining ingredients and pour into a mold pan.

3. Chill 3 to 4 hours. Unmold, slice, and serve.

Calories per serving: 68 – Fat: 0 – Sodium: 653 mg.
For exchange diets, count: 1 vegetable, 1/2 starch.
Preparation time: 20 minutes. – Chilling time: 4 hours.

Used with permission of the innkeepers at Bed and Breakfast on the Farm

Bed and Breakfast on the Farm

Bob & Sharon Cerv, Innkeepers
Route 2 Box 38
Leigh, Nebraska 68643
(402) 487-2482

This cozy farmhouse from the 30s is the place for hearty, home-cooked breakfasts, which include fresh Czech kolaches and strudel, breakfast casseroles, fruit, and beverages. Guest may dine in the country dining room or on the open porch. Quiet, clean country air, a variety of flowers, and a lazy pond await visitors. This recipe is a very unique ingredient combination and is requested by many.

Casual Corners Bed and Breakfast

Glenn & Ruth Lehman, Innkeepers
301 North Broad Street
Lititz, Pennsylvania 17543
(717) 626-5299;
Toll free: (800) 464-6764

Whatever Glenn and Ruth prepare, it will be different and delicious. Historic Lititz offers visitors the oldest pretzel bakery in the United States and Wilber Chocolate Factory. It is close to Lancaster in Amish country and all of the great outlet shopping there.

MANDARIN ORANGE SALAD
12 1/2-cup servings

20-ounce can pineapple chunks in juice
15-ounce can mandarin oranges in juice
3-ounce package tapioca pudding mix
3-ounce package cook-and-serve
  sugar-free vanilla pudding mix

6-ounce jar maraschino cherries,
  drained
2 medium firm bananas, sliced

1. Drain pineapple and oranges, reserving juices in a glass measuring cup. Set fruit aside.

2. Add water to juices to equal 3 cups; pour into a saucepan. Add pudding mixes; cook over medium heat, stirring constantly, until thick and bubbly, about 5 to 10 minutes.

3. Remove from heat; cool.

4. Place pineapple, oranges, and cherries in a 2-quart bowl. Pour pudding over and stir to coat. Chill for several hours. Add bananas just before serving.

Calories per serving: 96 – Fat: 0 – Sodium: 32 mg.
For exchange diets, count: 1 1/2 fruit.
Preparation time: 15 minutes.

Used with permission of the innkeepers at Casual Corners Bed and Breakfast

TANGY VEGETABLE SALAD
12 3/4-cup servings

1 cup chopped green peppers
8 green onions with tops, chopped
8-ounce can LeSueur English peas,
    drained (may substitute other peas)
1 cup chopped celery
16-ounce can shoepeg corn, drained
1 small pimento, chopped
16-ounce can seasoned French-cut
    green beans, drained

DRESSING:
3/4 cup apple cider vinegar
2 tablespoons oil
1 teaspoon salt
1 cup sugar
1 teaspoon pepper

1. Combine all vegetables in a large bowl.

2. Mix ingredients for the dressing in a saucepan, and heat just to a boil. Cool to room temperature and pour over vegetables. This salad is best if marinated at least 4 hours. Drain off marinade when serving.

Calories per serving: 103 – Fat: 1 g. – Sodium: 251 mg.
For exchange diets, count: 1 starch, 1 vegetable.
Preparation time: 20 minutes. Marinating time: 4 hours.

Used with permission of the innkeepers at A Bed and Breakfast on Maple

A Bed and Breakfast on Maple

Nonnie & Roy Fahsholtz, Innkeepers
P.O. Box 327
102 South Maple Street
Cortez, Colorado 81321
(970) 565-3906;
Toll free: (800) 665-3906

A Bed and Breakfast on Maple is a unique Rocky Mountain log and rock house where guests can relax with a warm western Colorado welcome. Nonnie loves to serve a warm, hearty breakfast every morning.

FRUIT SALAD FOR THE FINICKY
12 1-cup servings

16-ounce can fruit cocktail in juice,
    drained
2 bananas, sliced
1 pint fresh raspberries or strawberries,
    sliced

1 cup mini marshmallows
1 cup nonfat strawberry or
    raspberry yogurt
2 cups nonfat whipped topping

1. Fold all ingredients together gently and chill.

Calories per serving: 126 – Fat: 0 – Sodium: 35 mg.
For exchange diets, count: 2 fruit.
Preparation time: 10 minutes.

Used with permission of the innkeepers at The Claytonian (see page 57)

WALDORF SALAD
12 3/4-cup servings

DRESSING:
1/4 cup sugar
1 tablespoon flour
1/2 cup evaporated skim milk
1 teaspoon margarine
1/2 cup pineapple juice
8-ounce carton nonfat whipped topping

SALAD:
5 red and yellow Delicious apples,
  diced (unpeeled)
8-ounce can pineapple tidbits, drained
1 cup seedless red or green grapes
  cut in half
1/4 cup chopped walnuts

1. Mix sugar, flour, milk, margarine, and juice together with a whisk in a saucepan. Cook until boiling. Cool, then refrigerate for at least 1 hour. Fold in whipped topping.

2. Combine fruits in a large bowl. Fold in dressing until it covers to suit your taste. Add nuts just before serving to avoid turning fruit dark.

Calories per serving: 122 – Fat: 2 g. – Sodium: 2 mg.
For exchange diets, count: 2 fruit.
Preparation time: 15 minutes. – Refrigeration time: 1 hour

Used with permission of the innkeeper at Blue Spruce Inn

Blue Spruce Inn

Marvin & JoAnne Brown, Innkeepers
677 South 3rd Street
Lander, Wyoming 82520
(307) 332-8253;
Toll free: (888) 503-3311;
Fax: (307) 332-8253

Surrounded by giant blue spruce trees, this large brick house of 1920 reminds guests of a visit to grandma's house. Originally built in the era known as "Arts and Crafts," all rooms are now decorated with objects gathered during the hosts' global travels in the air force. Start your day with a sumptuous full breakfast and discover the unique recipes collected by your hosts. Sip coffee or tea in the evening on the porch swing or in the sun room at a bistro table. During your stay you can cast a fishing line in a mountain stream one block from the front porch, enjoy the fireplace on a cool evening, or play in the recreation room that provides a pool table, dart board, and wet bar.

STEAMED FRESH ASPARAGUS
WITH WARM TOMATO VINAIGRETTE
8 1-cup servings

8 cups your favorite combination of
the following, sliced:
fresh asparagus pieces
mushrooms
zucchini
broccoli
carrots
celery
yellow squash
cauliflower

WARM TOMATO VINAIGRETTE:
1 tablespoon olive oil
1/4 cup minced shallots
1 cup diced fresh tomatoes, peeled
and seeded
1/4 cup red wine vinegar
1 clove garlic, minced
2/3 cup dry white wine
1/2 teaspoon salt
1/2 teaspoon freshly ground black
pepper
1-2 tablespoons capers, optional

1. Heat oil in skillet and add shallots. Cook over low heat until wilted, about 5 minutes. Do not brown. Add 1/2 cup tomatoes and simmer 3 to 5 minutes. Add vinegar, garlic, wine, salt, and pepper. Simmer another 15 to 20 minutes until reduced to a thick sauce. Correct seasonings; stir in remaining tomatoes and capers.

2. Steam or cook fresh vegetables until crisp tender. Serve immediately with a teaspoon or two of vinaigrette on top.

Calories per serving: 37 – Fat: 1 g. – Sodium: 269 mg.
For exchange diets, count: 1 vegetable.
Preparation time: 30 minutes.

Used with permission of the innkeepers at The Inn at Merridun (see page 174)

Highlawn Inn

Sandra Kauffman, Innkeeper
304 Market Street
Berkeley Springs, West Virginia 25411
(304) 258-5700;
Toll free: (800) CALL-WVA (225-5982)

Highlawn Inn, a Victorian charmer, was built in the late 1890s by Algernon R. Unger for his bride, Chaffie Ziler. Breakfast finds delectable aromas wafting from Sandy's kitchen, where she is known for her ethereally light scrambled eggs, crisp bacon, dilled potatoes, homemade fresh croissants, fresh-squeezed orange juice, and other specialties. The ornate fireplace graces Highlawn Inn's intimate dining and sitting area, the tasteful setting for these opulent breakfasts. Snacks and springwater-based beverages are always available.

CONFETTI-HERB SQUASH
8 2/3-cup servings

2 cups yellow squash, cooked,
  mashed, and drained
2 eggs, well beaten
1/2 cup evaporated skim milk
1 tablespoon melted margarine
1 tablespoon sugar
1 tablespoon flour
3/4 cups grated Swiss cheese

salt and pepper to taste
2 tablespoons chopped fresh tarragon
1 tablespoon chopped fresh basil
1/2 cup chopped onions
1/4 cup chopped red peppers
1/4 cup chopped green peppers
1/2 cup bread crumbs

1. Preheat oven to 350°.

2. Combine all ingredients except bread crumbs in order given; mix well. Pour into greased glass casserole dish. Top with bread crumbs.

3. Bake for about an hour or until center is set. This dish adapts well to being doubled, made ahead and baked the next day, or baked and frozen. Defrost and reheat, covered with foil.

Calories per serving: 87 – Fat: 4 g. – Sodium: 92 mg.
For exchange diets, count: 2 vegetable, 1 fat.
Preparation time: 15 minutes. – Baking time: 1 hour.

Used with permission of the innkeeper at Highlawn Inn

BREADED TOMATOES
8 servings

4 tomatoes
1/4 teaspoon salt
1/4 teaspoon pepper
1/2 cup fine bread crumbs
1/2 cup grated Parmesan cheese

2 tablespoons chopped green chives
1 teaspoon dried basil
1 tablespoon reduced-fat margarine,
  melted

1. Preheat oven to 350°.

2. Cut tomatoes in half; sprinkle a little salt and pepper over them.

3. Mix bread crumbs, Parmesan cheese, chives, and basil in a small bowl. Pour melted butter into mix. Mix thoroughly.

4. Spoon crumb mixture onto tomatoes.

5. Bake 15 to 20 minutes, or until top is golden.

Calories per serving: 74 – Fat: 2 g. – Sodium: 243 mg.
For exchange diets, count: 1 starch.
Preparation time: 10 minutes. – Baking time: 20 minutes.

Used with permission of the innkeepers at The Hawkesdene House Bed & Breakfast Inn and Cottages (see page 46)

* * *

Desserts

APRICOT-LEMON BUNDT CAKE
18 slices

18-ounce package fat-free yellow
    cake mix
4 eggs or 1 cup liquid egg substitute
1 teaspoon lemon extract
3-ounce box sugar-free lemon gelatin
3/4 cup apricot nectar

3 tablespoons vegetable oil
1/2 cup nonfat sour cream

GLAZE:
2 tablespoons lemon juice
6 tablespoons powdered sugar

1. Preheat oven to 325°.

2. Spray a Bundt pan with nonstick cooking spray.

3. Combine all cake ingredients in a large mixing bowl. Blend with an electric mixer 3 minutes. Pour into prepared pan. Bake 45 to 50 minutes or until done. Remove cake from pan.

4. Mix together glaze ingredients.

5. While cake is hot, poke holes in the top with a fork and pour the glaze over the cake.

Calories per serving: 148 fat: 2 g. – Sodium: 240 mg.
For exchange diets, count: 1 starch, 1 fruit.
Preparation time: 10 minutes. – Baking time: 50 minutes.

Used with permission of the innkeepers at Riverwalk Inn

Riverwalk Inn

Tracy & Jan Hammer, Proprietors
Johnny Halpenny & Tammy Hill, Innkeepers
329 Old Guilbeau
San Antonio, Texas 78204
(210) 212-8300;
Toll free: (800) 254-4440;
Fax: (210) 229-9422

Follow the old Mission Trail along the banks of the San Antonio River to the spot where authentic 19th-century two-story log homes stand nestled among native pecan and poplar trees. The Riverwalk Inn's mission is to have guests relive the history of the old San Antonio through the lifestyle of our Tennessee brothers, Davy Crockett and James Bowie, who fought for Texas independence at the Battle of the Alamo. Jan's granny used to make this cake on Friday nights. Riverwalk Inn guests love it.

BIRDSEED CAKE
18 slices

nonstick cooking spray
3 cups all-purpose flour
1 teaspoon baking soda
1 teaspoon cinnamon
1 1/2 cups sugar
1 teaspoon salt
1/4 cup oil

3/4 cup nonfat sour cream
8-ounce can crushed pineapple
    with juice
1 1/2 teaspoons vanilla
3 eggs or 3/4 cup liquid egg substitute
2 large bananas, diced
1/4 cup pecans, chopped

1. Preheat oven to 350°.

2. Spray a tube pan with cooking spray.

3. Mix dry ingredients together in a large mixing bowl. Add remaining ingredients. Mix together, but do not beat.

4. Pour into prepared pan and bake for 1 hour and 20 minutes. Cool cake for 20 minutes, then turn out onto cake plate and cool to room temperature.

HUMMINGBIRD FROSTING:

8 ounces nonfat cream cheese,
    softened

1 cup powdered sugar
8 ounces nonfat whipped topping

1. Mix cream cheese and powdered sugar together in a mixing bowl. Fold in whipped topping. Frost cooled cake.

Calories per serving: 233 – Fat: 5 g. – Sodium: 220 mg.
For exchange diets, count: 1 1/2 starch, 1 fruit, 1 fat.
Preparation time: 20 minutes. – Baking time: 1 hour, 20 minutes.
Cooling time: 1 hour.

Used with permission of the innkeepers at Hilton's Bluff Bed & Breakfast Inn (see page 39)

LEMON WALNUT BREAKFAST CAKE
20 slices

nonstick cooking spray
6 tablespoons margarine
1 1/4 cups sugar
4 eggs or 1 cup liquid egg substitute
6 tablespoons nonfat sour cream
3/4 cup buttermilk
2 1/4 cups flour

1/4 teaspoon soda
1/4 teaspoon salt
grated rind of 1 fresh lemon
1/2 cup chopped walnuts
GLAZE:
juice of 1 lemon
1/4 cup sugar

1. Preheat oven to 350°.

2. Spray a Bundt cake pan generously with cooking spray.

3. In a large mixing bowl, cream margarine with sugar. Add eggs one at a time, mixing well between additions. Stir in sour cream and buttermilk.

4. Add flour, soda, and salt and mix again. Fold in lemon rind and walnuts.

5. Bake for 35 minutes or until cake tests done. Cool for 15 minutes, then turn out onto cooling rack.

6. To glaze: combine lemon juice and sugar. Poke holes in the top of the cake and pour glaze slowly into the cake. Cover and enjoy for 3 days.

Calories per serving: 167 – Fat: 5 g. – Sodium: 105 mg.
For exchange diets, count: 2 starch.
Preparation time: 15 minutes. – Baking time: 35 minutes.
Cooling time: 15 minutes.

Used with permission of the innkeeper at Abigail's "Elegant Victorian Mansion" (see page 12)

CHOCOLATE ZUCCHINI CAKE
24 squares

nonstick cooking spray
1/2 cup margarine
1 3/4 cups sugar
1/2 cup nonfat sour cream
2 eggs or 1/2 cup liquid egg substitute
1 teaspoon vanilla
2 1/2 cups flour

1/4 cup cocoa
1/2 teaspoon baking powder
1/2 teaspoon salt
1 teaspoon soda
1 teaspoon cinnamon
2 cups grated zucchini
1/2 cup chocolate chips

1. Preheat oven to 325°. Spray a 9 x 13-inch baking pan with cooking spray.

2. In a large mixing bowl, cream margarine, sugar, and sour cream. Add eggs and vanilla, and beat well. Stir in flour, cocoa, baking powder, salt, soda, and cinnamon. Fold in zucchini and chocolate chips.

3. Spread batter in the prepared pan.

4. Bake for 50 minutes or until cake tests done with toothpick.

Calories per serving: 149 – Fat: 4 g. – Sodium: 122 mg.
For exchange diets, count: 1 starch, 1/2 fruit, 1 fat.
Preparation time: 20 minutes. – Baking time: 50 minutes.

Used with permission of the innkeeper at Calmar Guesthouse (see page 76)

PEACH CREAM BREAKFAST CAKE
12 squares

nonstick cooking spray
29-ounce can peach halves in juice
8-ounce package reduced-fat
    cream cheese, softened
1/4 cup all-fruit apricot or peach
    preserves

9-ounce box yellow cake mix
2 tablespoons vegetable oil
1 egg or 1/4 cup liquid egg
    substitute
1 teaspoon ginger

1. Preheat oven to 350°.

2. Spray an 8-inch square pan with cooking spray.

3. Drain peaches, reserving 1/2 cup juice. Slice peaches and place into the prepared pan.

4. In a small mixing bowl, beat cheese and preserves until smooth. Pour over peaches.

5. Beat cake mix, reserved peach juice, oil, egg, and ginger. Pour over peaches. Bake 35 to 40 minutes.

Calories per serving: 152 – Fat: 5 mg. – Sodium: 217 mg.
For exchange diets, count: 1 starch, 1/2 fruit, 1 fat.
Preparation time: 15 minutes. – Baking time: 40 minutes.

Used with permission of the innkeepers at Cinnamon Hill Bed & Breakfast (see page 135)

CHERRY CHEESE PIE
10 slices

8 ounces 50% reduced-fat
  cream cheese, room temperature
1/4 cup powdered sugar
1 cup nonfat whipped topping

9-inch prepared graham cracker crust
20-ounce can reduced-sugar cherry
  pie filling

1. Soften cream cheese in a mixing bowl with a fork. Beat in powdered sugar. Fold in whipped topping. Turn into prepared crust.

2. With a slotted spoon, spoon cherries over the pie. Chill for 2 hours. Slice and serve.

Calories per serving: 191 – Fat: 9 g. – Sodium: 197 mg.
For exchange diets, count: 1 starch, 1/2 fruit, 2 fat.
Preparation time: 10 minutes. Chilling time: 2 hours.

Used with permission of the innkeepers at The Claytonian (see page 57)

WINE CAKE
16 slices

18-ounce package reduced-fat
  yellow cake mix
3-ounce package instant vanilla
  pudding mix
4 eggs or 1 cup liquid egg substitute

1 teaspoon nutmeg
3/4 cup sherry
1/4 cup oil
1/2 cup nonfat sour cream

1. Preheat oven to 350°.

2. Spray Bundt pan generously with nonstick cooking spray.

3. Combine all ingredients in a large mixing bowl. Beat for 3 minutes, then pour into prepared pan.

4. Bake for 55 to 60 minutes. When cake is cool, sprinkle with powdered sugar and serve with fruit topping.

Calories per serving: 144 – Fat: 2 g. – Sodium: 233 mg.
For exchange diets, count: 1 starch, 1 fruit.
Preparation time: 10 minutes. – Baking time: 60 minutes.

Used with permission of the innkeepers at The Claytonian (see page 57)

LEMON CURD CHEESECAKE
16 slices

FILLING:
1 cup sugar
16 ounces reduced-fat cream cheese
3 eggs or 3/4 cup liquid egg substitute
juice from 2 fresh lemons
1 1/2 teaspoons vanilla
1/4 teaspoon salt
3 cups nonfat sour cream

LEMON CURD:
1/2 cup sugar
4 whole eggs or 1 cup liquid egg substitute
juice from 2 1/2 lemons
2 tablespoons unsalted margarine

CRUST:
2 tablespoons melted margarine
1 cup crushed graham cracker crumbs
    or leftover muffin crumbs

1. Cream the sugar and cream cheese until sugar dissolves and mixture is light and creamy. Add three eggs, one at a time, until incorporated.

2. Mix in lemon juice, vanilla, salt, and sour cream. Mix thoroughly. Chill.

3. Mix together ingredients for the crust and press into the bottom of a springform pan.

4. Preheat oven to 275°.

5. Transfer chilled mixture into the springform pan and bake for 1 hour and 15 minutes. Turn off oven and leave cheesecake inside for an additional 30 minutes to set. Remove and chill.

6. To make lemon curd: Whip sugar and eggs together over low heat in a small saucepan, taking care not to let the mixture curdle.

7. Add lemon juice and margarine and continue to mix over low heat until mixture firms. Chill and use for topping of cheesecake.

Calories per slice: 240 – Fat: 9 g. – Sodium: 327 mg.
For exchange diets, count: 1 starch, 1/2 skim milk, 1 fruit, 1 fat.
Preparation time: 10 minutes – Baking time: 1 hour, 15 minutes
Setting time in oven: 30 minutes – Chilling time: 1 hour

Used with permission of the innkeepers at Camden Harbour Inn (see page 150)

BLUEBERRY SOUR CREAM PIE
10 slices

1 reduced-fat graham cracker crust,
 unbaked
FILLING:
1 cup nonfat sour cream
1 egg or 1/4 cup liquid egg substitute
1/3 cup sugar
1/4 cup flour
1 teaspoon almond or lemon extract

2 cups fresh or frozen
 blueberries
1 tablespoon flour
TOPPING:
1/2 cup flour
2 tablespoons soft margarine
3 tablespoons sugar
2 tablespoons sliced almonds

1. Preheat oven to 350°.

2. Mix all filling ingredients except blueberries and flour. Toss blueberries with flour and fold into sour cream mixture. Pour into crust.

3. Bake until filling is just setting, about 25 to 30 minutes.

4. Place flour, margarine, and sugar in food processor or blender and pulse on and off until crumbly. Add sliced almonds and pulse briefly. Sprinkle topping mixture over pies, and bake another 12 to 15 minutes. Cool to near room temperature before serving; refrigerate unused portions.

Calories per slice: 200 – Fat: 5 g. – Sodium 200 mg.
For exchange diets, count: 2 fruit, 1/2 skim milk, 1 fat.
Preparation time: 20 minutes. – Baking time: 45 minutes.

Used with permission of the innkeepers at The Inn at Merridun (see page 174)

NEARLY GUILT-FREE PINEAPPLE CHEESE TOAST

12 servings, 1 sandwich each

1 cup low-calorie apricot preserves
1/2 cup low-fat ricotta cheese
8 ounces reduced-fat cream cheese
20-ounce can juice-packed crushed
    pineapple, drained very well
1 loaf French bread

EGG MIXTURE:
1 teaspoon vanilla
1 cup milk
4 beaten eggs or 1 cup liquid
    egg substitute
1/2 teaspoon nutmeg
1 tablespoon sugar

1. Preheat oven to 325°.

2. In a mixing bowl, combine the preserves, cheeses, and drained pineapple.

3. Slice French bread into 3/4-inch slices (about 24 slices). Generously coat half of the slices with cheese mixture. Top with the second slice of bread.

4. Combine ingredients for egg mixture in a shallow dish.

5. Generously spray a nonstick skillet or griddle with nonstick cooking spray. Preheat to medium heat.

6. Coat each side of the sandwich in egg mixture and brown lightly on griddle.

7. Place browned sandwiches on foil-lined baking sheet. Bake for 20 minutes. Serve with praline syrup or apricot preserves.

Calories per serving: 223 – Fat: 6 g. – Sodium: 319 mg.
For exchange diets, count: 2 starch, 1 lean meat.
Preparation time: 25 minutes. – Baking time: 20 minutes.

Used with permission of the innkeepers at Cameron's Crag Bed & Breakfast

Cameron's Crag Bed & Breakfast

Kay & Glen Cameron, Innkeepers
P.O. Box 526
Point Lookout, Missouri 65726
(417) 335-8134;
Toll free: (800) 933-8529 (reservations)

This special bed and breakfast is a contemporary home perched high on a bluff overlooking Lake Taneycomo and the Branson skyline. Beautiful scenery, hearty breakfasts, and delightful accommodations will make your Branson vacation a getaway to remember. Kay has drawn from her knowledge of foods and an Ozark heritage to compile a delicious collection of old family recipes and Ozark dishes.

PEACH & BLUEBERRY BREAKFAST PIE
8 servings

nonstick cooking spray
3 large eggs or 3/4 cup liquid
  egg substitute
6 tablespoons sugar
1/3 cup evaporated skim milk

1 teaspoon vanilla extract
3 tablespoons flour
2 ripe peaches, sliced
3/4 cup fresh or frozen blueberries
powdered sugar

1. Preheat oven to 375°.

2. Spray a shallow 9-inch pie pan with cooking spray.

3. Combine eggs and sugar in a bowl, and beat with an electric mixer until frothy. Add evaporated skim milk, vanilla, and flour, and beat until smooth.

4. Pour into prepared pie pan enough batter to coat bottom. Set the remaining batter aside. Bake for 5 minutes.

5. Remove from oven and scatter fruit over batter. Pour remaining batter over it and bake until set, about 20 to 25 minutes.

6. Remove from oven. Cool 30 minutes, then dust with powdered sugar. Cut into 8 wedges and serve.

Calories per slice: 95 – Fat: 1 g. – Sodium: 56 mg.
For exchange diets, count: 1 1/2 fruit.
Preparation time: 15 minutes. – Baking time: 30 minutes.
Cooling time: 30 minutes.

Used with permission of the innkeeper at Holly Hill House Bed & Breakfast (see page 178)

Raspberry Custard Brûlée
4 servings

2 cups fresh raspberries (1 pint)
2 tablespoons sugar
2 teaspoons cornstarch
1 egg, lightly beaten, or 1/4 cup liquid
  egg substitute

1 cup skim milk
2 tablespoons low-fat sour cream
1/2 teaspoon vanilla extract
4 teaspoons brown sugar

1. Gently rinse raspberries; drain. Divide raspberries evenly among four 6-ounce ovenproof ramekins or custard cups; set aside.

2. Combine sugar and cornstarch in a small saucepan; stir well. Add egg; stir well. Gradually add milk, stirring well. Cook over low heat 12 minutes or until thickened, stirring constantly. Remove from heat; let cool 5 minutes. Fold in sour cream and vanilla; stir well.

3. Spoon custard mixture evenly over raspberries.

4. Place ramekins on a baking sheet. Sprinkle each with 1 teaspoon brown sugar.

5. Broil 4 to 5 inches from heat 2 minutes or until sugar melts. Serve warm.

Calories per serving: 118 – Fat: 1 g. – Sodium: 70 mg.
For exchange diets, count: 1 fruit, 1/2 skim milk.
Preparation time: 20 minutes. – Broiling time: 2 minutes.

Used with permission of the innkeepers at Romancing the Past Bed & Breakfast (see page 53)

Creamy Rice Pudding
16 1/2-cup servings

5 cups water
2 teaspoons salt
1 tablespoon margarine
1 pound long-grain rice
3 cups skim milk

1 cup sugar
2 eggs, beaten, or 1/2 cup liquid
  egg substitute
Serve with cinnamon, sugar, and
  cream

1. Bring water to boil in a large saucepan. Add salt, margarine, and rice.

2. Cover and simmer for 20 minutes or until the water is absorbed.

3. Stir in milk, sugar, and eggs. Reduce heat to simmer and cook for 10 minutes.

4. Portion into dessert dishes and serve with cinnamon, sugar, and cream on the side.

Calories per serving: 162 – Fat: 1 g. – Sodium: 315 mg.
For exchange diets, count: 2 starch.
Preparation time: 5 minutes. – Cooking time: 30 minutes.

Used with permission of the innkeepers at Eagles' Landing Bed and Breakfast (see page 52)

BREAD PUDDING (BROTPUDDING)

16 squares

nonstick cooking spray
10 slices white bread
  (preferably homemade)
10 slices brown bread
  (preferably homemade)
6 tablespoons sugar
1 tablespoon butter-flavored margarine
14-ounce can evaporated skim milk
1 tablespoon flour

1 large Golden Delicious apple,
  peeled, seeded, and chopped
1 tablespoon raisins
1/2 teaspoon cinnamon
1/2 teaspoon grated orange rind
1/2 teaspoon lemon juice
2 tablespoons chopped nuts
2 teaspoons rum extract

1. Spray an 11 x 7-inch baking dish with cooking spray.

2. Break bread into small pieces and spread evenly in prepared dish.

3. Mix all remaining ingredients together, and pour over bread.

4. Cover, refrigerate, and let soak for 1 hour.

5. Preheat oven to 350°. Bake for 45 minutes or until top is light brown.

Calories per serving: 153 – Fat: 3 g. – Sodium: 194 mg.
For exchange diets, count: 1 starch, 1 fruit.
Preparation time: 20 minutes. – Soaking time: 1 hour – Baking time: 45 minutes.

*Used with permission of the innkeepers at Flemingsburg House Bed & Breakfast
at Sweetwater Farm (see page 6)*

Salisbury House

Cathryn & Mary Wiese, Innkeepers
750 16th Avenue East
Seattle, Washington 98112
(206) 328-8682;
Fax: (206) 720-1019
E-mail: Cathy@salisburyhouse.com

Salisbury House offers gracious in-city accommodations to the discerning traveler. A full breakfast featuring seasonal fruits and fresh baked muffins and breads is served in the sunny dining room.

BAKED BLINTZ

12 squares

The innkeepers have graciously shared this recipe many times. It makes a great brunch dish and it can be assembled the night before, refrigerated and baked in the morning. And it's full of calcium!

nonstick cooking spray
flour

FILLING:
6-ounce package reduced-fat
   cream cheese (room temperature)
1 cup low-fat cottage cheese
1 egg, beaten
1 tablespoon sugar
1 teaspoon vanilla

BATTER:
1/4 cup margarine
1/3 cup sugar
4 eggs
1 cup flour
2 teaspoons baking soda
1/2 cup nonfat sour cream
1 cup nonfat plain yogurt
1/2 cup orange juice

GARNISH: nonfat sour cream and fresh
   raspberry preserves

1. Preheat oven to 375°.

2. Spray a 9 x 13-inch baking pan with cooking spray. Sprinkle with flour to coat.

3. In a small bowl, beat cream cheese; add cottage cheese, egg, sugar, and vanilla. Mix well and set aside.

4. In a large bowl, cream margarine and sugar. Add eggs one at a time, beating well. Add flour and baking soda. Mix in sour cream and yogurt; add orange juice.

5. Pour half of batter into prepared pan. Add filling and then top with remaining batter.

6. Bake 45 to 50 minutes or until lightly browned. Slice into 12 squares and garnish with a dollop of nonfat sour cream and fresh raspberry preserves.

Calories per serving: 218 – Fat: 5 g. – Sodium: 432 mg.
For exchange diets, count: 1 starch, 1 skim milk, 1 fat.
Preparation time: 15 minutes. – Baking time: 50 minutes.

Used with permission of the innkeepers at Salisbury House

BRANDY CHERRIES CHAMBORD

6 4-ounce servings

2 tablespoons margarine
1/2 cup sugar
juice of 1 lemon
1 cup cherry juice
juice of 1 orange

16-ounce can pitted and drained
cherries
2 ounces Chambord or cherry-flavored
liqueur
1 ounce brandy

1. Over low heat, combine margarine and sugar in saucepan until golden. Add lemon, cherry, and orange juices and cook until smooth.

2. Add cherries and Chambord and simmer for a few more minutes.

3. Add the brandy and ignite. Bring to the table and serve with ladle over crepes or pancakes or as a topping for ice cream or cheesecake.

Calories per serving: 150 – Fat: 4 g. – Sodium: 58 mg.
For exchange diets, count: 1 1/2 fruit, 1 fat.
Preparation time: 15 minutes.

Used with permission of the innkeepers at Lakeshore Bed & Breakfast

Lakeshore Bed & Breakfast

Dan & Jackie Hansen, Innkeepers
11001 Lakeshore
West Olive, Michigan 49460
(616) 844-2697;
Toll free: (800) 342-6736;
Fax: (616) 844-2698

This fully restored 4,500-square-foot mansion was built in 1935 on 275 feet of private Lake Michigan beach frontage. Guests enjoy strolling through the history of American Presidents with the innkeepers' unique collection of historical documents and memorabilia. The Hansens offer 24-hour beverage service, evening sherry, and a full gourmet breakfast served on Lincoln or Washington White House china.

MANGO COBBLER, ANY DAY, ANY WAY

8 squares

1 cup all-purpose flour
1 tablespoon baking powder
1/2 teaspoon salt
4-ounce can evaporated skim milk
1 egg, beaten, or 1/4 cup liquid
    egg substitute

2 tablespoons margarine
2 fresh mangoes
1/4 cup sugar
1 teaspoon cinnamon

1. Preheat oven to 350°.

2. Mix flour, baking powder, and salt together in a mixing bowl. Add milk and beaten egg; mix into a smooth batter.

3. Melt margarine in shallow 8-inch square baking pan. Pour batter over margarine.

4. Peel mangoes; slice and sprinkle over batter. Sprinkle with sugar and cinnamon.

5. Bake for 40 to 45 minutes. Top will be lightly browned and the center will be firm.

Calories per serving: 129 – Fat: 3 g. – Sodium: 191 mg.
For exchange diets, count: 1 fruit, 1 starch.
Preparation time: 15 minutes. – Baking time: 45 minutes.

Used with permission of the innkeepers at Seminole Country Inn

Seminole Country Inn

Jonnie Williams & Sheri Hubbard, Innkeepers
15885 Southwest Warfield Boulevard
Indiantown, Florida 34956
(561) 597-3777;
Fax: (561) 597-4691

Since 1926, there's been a mystique that remains unique to the Seminole Country Inn. Its pleasant surroundings bring back a sense of an old Florida that only a special few get to experience again. The twilight grandeur of the old South is captured as guests enter through grand double French doors into the main lobby. The innkeepers comment this recipe is always great for a happy crew; it feeds 6 to 8 mermaids.

Ashton Country House

Dorie & Vince DiStefano, Innkeepers
1205 Middlebrook Avenue
Staunton, Virginia 24401
(540) 885-7819;
Toll free: (800) 296-7819

A town where history lives, Staunton and the surrounding area offers something to entertain almost everyone. Enjoy the natural beauty of horses and cattle grazing in the pastures. Twenty-five acres of rolling land abound with magnificent views of the Blue Ridge Mountains. Guests revel in the grand scale of the Victorian mind set, as they relax in the elegant mansion built in 1860. Enjoy the lofty ceilings, 40-foot center hall, solid brick interior walls, and magnificent heartpine and maple floors.

PEAR CRISP IN THE MICROWAVE
4 1-cup servings

4 firm pears, cored and cut into
    12 wedges
1/4 cup apple jelly (or honey)
1/2 cup chopped walnuts

2 tablespoons quick cooking oats
2 tablespoons brown sugar
2 tablespoons melted margarine

1. Place pear slices in microwave-safe bowl.

2. Spoon apple jelly or honey on top. Sprinkle with nuts, oats, and sugar. Drizzle with margarine.

3. Microwave on high 6 minutes. Stir and cook 3 or 4 minutes more until pears are fork tender.

Calories per serving: 234 – Fat: 8 g. – Sodium: 42 mg.
For exchange diets, count: 1 starch, 2 fruit, 1 fat.
Preparation time: 10 minutes. – Microwave cooking time: 10 minutes.

Used with permission of the innkeepers at Ashton Country House

SPIRITED BAKED APPLE

4 servings

4 Granny Smith apples
1/4 cup brown sugar
1 tablespoon butter-flavored margarine
1/4 cup currants
2 tablespoons finely chopped nuts
1 teaspoon cinnamon

1 teaspoon ground allspice
1/3 cup water
2 tablespoons bourbon or
   2 teaspoons bourbon extract
Garnish: nonfat whipped topping

1. Preheat oven to 375°.

2. Wash apples, use a metal corer to remove seeds, and place in an 8- or 9-inch glass baking dish.

3. Fill the center of the apples with brown sugar and press down to pack. Dot with margarine; press down. Add a few currants and fine-ground nuts. Sprinkle with spices.

4. Pour water and bourbon into the dish. Bake for 1 hour or until apples are soft when pierced with a toothpick. Baste with juices every 15 minutes.

5. Serve apples warm in footed dishes with whipped topping.

Calories per serving: 213 – Fat: 7 g. – Sodium: 27 mg.
For exchange diets, count: 3 fruit, 1 fat.
Preparation time: 15 minutes. – Baking time: 60 minutes.

Used with permission of the innkeepers at The Log House & Homestead on Spirit Lake (see page 65)

BANANA BONANZA
12 servings

12 slices reduced-fat pound cake
  or 12 day-old muffins
SAUCE:
12-ounce can frozen pink lemonade or
  limeade concentrate

7-12 ripe bananas (depending on how
  thick a sauce desired)
2 cups chopped fruit
Garnish: fresh berries and fresh mint

1. In blender or food processor, combine lemonade concentrate with bananas; blend to desired consistency. Adjust tartness with additional fresh lemon or lime.

2. Add chopped fruit (almost any fruit is tasty) and refrigerate. The acid in the sauce will hold the fruit fresh for several days in the refrigerator.

3. For each serving, crumble a slice or two of pound cake or a muffin in a small, decorative dessert dish. Cover with fruit sauce, and garnish with seasonal berries and a sprig of mint.

Calories per slice: 238 – Fat: 1 g. – Sodium: 163 mg.
For exchange diets, count: 1 1/2 starch, 2 fruit.
Preparation time: 15 minutes.

Used with permission of the innkeeper at General Hooker's B & B

General Hooker's B & B

Lori Hall, Innkeeper
125 Southwest Hooker Street
Portland, Oregon 97201
(503) 222-4435;
Toll free: (800) 745-4135;
Fax: (503) 295-6410
E-mail ghbandb@teleport.com

General Hooker's Bed & Breakfast is a blend of Victorian charm, classic decor, quiet convenience, and creature comfort. When Lori found this house on Hooker Street in old South Portland, she knew it would be ideal for a bed and breakfast. An airy, mid-size Victorian on a tree-lined street in a Historical Conservation District, it is just a block from downtown Portland. All the streets of the area were named for Civil War generals, including "Fighting Joe" Hooker, a Union general from Hadley, Massachusetts. His name lives on because of his business-like handling of camp followers, known then as "Hooker's Second Army" (later shortened to its current usage). Breakfast features freshly ground coffee, fruit in season, and whole-grain breads, a bonus to the health-conscious guest.

OREGON BISCOTTI
48 biscotti

1 cup sugar
1/4 cup margarine, room temperature
1/4 cup nonfat sour cream
3 large eggs or 3/4 cup liquid
   egg substitute

1/4 cup sherry
3 cups flour
1 1/2 teaspoons baking powder
1/2 cup dried cranberries
1/4 cup chopped hazelnuts

1. Preheat oven to 375°.

2. Cream sugar, margarine, and sour cream in a large mixing bowl. Stir in eggs one at a time. Stir in sherry. Blend in flour and baking powder. Carefully fold in cranberries and hazelnuts.

3. Dough will be sticky. Form two loaves, 2 inches by 2 inches by 16 inches. Place on a baking sheet and bake for approximately 20 minutes. Cool.

4. Cut on pan into 3/4-inch slices; place flat side down. Bake for approximately 15 minutes. Store in airtight container or freezer.

Calories per serving: 62 – Fat: 1 g. – Sodium: 22 mg.
For exchange diets, count as: 1 starch.
Preparation time: 20 minutes. – Baking time: 35 minutes.

Used with permission of the innkeeper at Chetco River Inn

Chetco River Inn

Sandra Brogger, Innkeeper
21202 High Prairie Road
Brookings, Oregon 97415
(541) 670-1645;
Toll free: (800) 327-2688;
Fax: (503) 469-4341

The Chetco River Inn brings one to another world, a place where the lulling sound of river rushing over stone calms the city dweller and suburbanite alike. Breakfast might feature an omelet made with eggs supplied by a neighbor (a river guide who keeps two dozen chickens), breakfast meats such as English bangers or cottage bacon, crepe dishes, and breakfast muffins made with apples, hazelnuts, pecans, and carrots. If this fantasy fare isn't enough to last till dinner, guests help themselves to fruit and homemade chocolate or biscotti and tea, which are left out in the kitchen.

BUFFALO CHIP COOKIES
76 buffalo chips

nonstick cooking spray
1 cup reduced-fat margarine
1 cup nonfat sour cream
4 cups dark brown sugar
4 eggs
2 cups white sugar
2 teaspoons vanilla extract
4 cups flour

2 teaspoons baking powder
2 teaspoons baking soda
2 cups oatmeal
6-ounce package chocolate chips
1/4 cup chopped pecans or walnuts
2 cups Rice Krispies
1 cup coconut (optional)

1. Preheat oven to 350°. Spray a baking sheet with cooking spray.

2. In a very large bowl, cream margarine and sour cream. Add brown sugar, eggs, white sugar, and vanilla. Sift and add flour, baking powder, and baking soda. Add oatmeal, then stir in the chocolate chips, nuts, Rice Krispies, and coconut.

3. Form batter into buffalo chips (cookies), using approximately 1/4 cup batter per cookie. Put cookies on cookie sheet (9 cookies to a sheet).

4. Bake for about 12 to 15 minutes. Let cool 3 minutes before removing from baking sheet.

Calories per serving: 136 – Fat: 3 g. sodium: 87 mg.
For exchange diets, count: 1 starch, 1 fat.
Preparation time: 20 minutes. – Baking time: 15 minutes.

Used with permission of the innkeeper at Wilson House Inn Bed and Breakfast

Wilson House Inn Bed and Breakfast

Delissa Britt, Innkeeper
6312 Allen Road
Ocean Springs, Mississippi 39565
(228) 875-6933;
Toll free: (800) 872-6933;
Fax: (228) 875-6933
E-mail: wilsonbb@sunherald.infi.net

Originally located north of Gulfport, Mississippi, this two-story log house was home to Joel Pinson Wilson and his family. They were remembered for the acres of orange orchards they planted, thus the surrounding community became known as Orange Grove. The house was later relocated to Ocean Springs. Guests at this house rise to a full Southern-style home-cooked breakfast. Delicious homemade biscuits, ham, eggs, fresh fruit, coffee, and juices are served family style.

Index

E

Eagle River Inn, 112

Eagles' Landing Bed & Breakfast, 52

egg entrées
  Almond Supreme Omelet, 104
  Asiago & Asparagus Omelet, 104–105
  Baked Eggs in Cheesy Wild Rice, 126
  Best Ever Veggie Omelet, 107
  Breakfast in Bread, 124–125
  Breakfast Pie, 109–110
  Country Breakfast Pie, 111
  Creamy Scrambled Eggs, 106
  Crustless Ham and Egg Quiche, 110
  Dilled Eggs with Salmon, 107
  Eggs Derelict, 127
  Eggs Florentine, 130–131
  Egg Truffles, 129
  Egg Truffles with Canadian Bacon, 128
  Featherbed Eggs, 109
  Festive Egg Squares, 131
  Florentine Benedict, 133
  Garden Polenta Pie, 113
  Green Chile Quiche, 112
  Guesthouse Quiche, 114
  Ham and Egg Bake with Croutons, 135
  Hash Brown and Sausage Mini-Frittatas, 134
  Hoppel Poppel, 132
  Huevos Rancheros, 136
  Huevos Rojos Enchiladas, 139
  Newfoundland Frittata, 137
  One-Serving Cheese Puff, 138
  Overnight Grits & Sausage Casserole, 138
  Pesto Soufflé, 115
  Potato Omelet, 108
  Quiche Lorraine, 116
  Quickie Blender Quiche with Three Variations, 117
  Rosie's Eggs Mexicana, 140
  Russ's Ruffled Eggs, 141
  Saffron Cream Eggs, 142
  Sour Cream Soufflé, 118
  Spinach and Crab Quiche, 118–119
  Spinach & Eggs Greenbrier, 143
  Stitt House Breakfast Quiche, 119–120
  Summer Veggie Pie, 121
  Tarte d'Alsace, 145
  Toasted Almond Zucchini Quiche, 123
  Turkey and Broccoli Overnight Egg Bake, 144

Eggs Derelict, 127

Eggs Florentine, 130–131

Egg Truffles, 129

Egg Truffles with Canadian Bacon, 128

1874 Stonehouse Bed & Breakfast on Mulberry Hill, 62

Electric Griddle Puffed French Toast, 98

F

Fat-Free Home Fries, 149

Featherbed Eggs, 109

Festive Egg Squares, 131

Finnish Heritage Homestead Bed & Breakfast, 127

fish
  Chinook Salmon on the Barbecue Grill, 175
  Crabmeat Dip, 15
  Crab Puffs, 21
  Fish Kabobs, 173
  Fish Veracruz, 174
  Puffed Crab Roll, 19–20
  Smoked Salmon Mousse, 12